BEHIND THE COURTYARD DOOR

The Daily Life of Tribeswomen in Northern Morocco

The author in traditional married woman's dress, at the time of her stay among the Aith Waryaghar tribe in the Moroccan Rif
(Photograph by David Montgomery Hart)

URSULA KINGSMILL HART

BEHIND THE COURTYARD DOOR

The Daily Life of Tribeswomen in Northern Morocco

THE IPSWICH PRESS
Ipswich, Massachusetts

Also by Ursula Kingsmill Hart: *Two Ladies of Colonial Algeria: The Lives and Times of Aurélie Picard and Isabelle Eberhardt,* Ohio University Monographs in International Studies, Africa Series, No. 49 (Athens: University of Ohio Press, 1987).

Photographs by Ursula Kingsmill Hart and David Montgomery Hart. Drawings by Ursula Kingsmill Hart.

Front cover: Bride and her friends setting out to issue wedding invitations.

 ISBN 0-938864-18-1

Manufactured in the United States of America by Bradford & Bigelow, Inc., Danvers, MA 01923. Published by:

THE IPSWICH PRESS
Box 291
Ipswich, Massachusetts 01938

Author's Dedication

This book is dedicated, first, to Muhand and to the various women of his extended family, in both the upper and lower houses; secondly, to Dave, with love, for having made it all possible; and finally, but not least, to my children, Carrol, Christine and Stephen, who sometimes accompanied me but who always had to put up with so much.

Author's illustrated map of the area described in her book

Contents

Introduction: What Social Anthropology Is All About *1*

1. New Territory *5*

2. Housework *12*

3. Getting to Know Them; Sacrifice of the Fatted Calf *24*

4. The Wedding Walk. . . And Not a Thing to Wear *32*

5. Striptease and Dancing *45*

6. Prenuptial Ritual *56*

7. The Daily Round — A Pressure Cooker Is a Fearsome Thing *66*

8. Ophthalmic Surgery *82*

9. Bathing and Birth Control *87*

10. A Barren Woman Leads a Woeful Life *95*

11. The Women Up the Hill *105*

12. A Woman's Place Is In the Home *119*

13. It Is God's Will — Marriage, Sex and Legends *129*

14. Birth and Baby Care *140*

15. Death. . . and Farewell *147*

16. Epilogue *160*

Illustrations

I. Photographs taken at the Lower House in the Nkur River community of r-'Attaf: *Grouped between pages 31 and 32*

Muhand's house; valley viewed from the cave lavatory
Close-up of Muhand's house; inside Muhand's courtyard
Muhand; Khadduj, his third wife; Arhimu, his mother
Dhamimund, Rwazna and Arhimu
Hmid, with his head being squeezed; Dris ("l'Amirikani")
The author with Muhand and two of his children

II. Photographs of the wedding of Arqiya, Muhand's niece: *Grouped between pages 65 and 66*

Bride and bridesmaids; bridal party at the courtyard door
Arqiya's bridesmaids
The bride dancing in the courtyard
The bride with her closest friends; arrival of the musicians
The chief drummer
Bridal mule carpeted up; final pinnings before going away

III. Photographs taken at the Upper House in the mountain community of l-'Ass: *Grouped between pages 118 and 119*

Bu Tahar Uzarqan; Fadhma, his wife; corner of their house
Hadduma, Muhand's first wife, with two daughters
One of the unmarried sisters; Mimuna's shy daughters
'Aisha's small daughter
Arqiya, Muhand's frivolous daughter
Maghniya before the scorpion sting
Olive wood, mortar and pestle; Dhamimund, water jugs
The valley of the spring
Plowing a steep hill; Hmid herding goats
The bridegroom; Muhand learning to use a camera
Tea drinking during a plowing break

Introduction: What Social Anthropology Is All About

The cave was the communal lavatory and had a glorious wind-swept view across the valley below. I was squatting there, thinking about nothing in particular, when *Zing! Gdoyng!* a wasp got me dead on target—you know where! With a yell I leaped to my feet, pulled up my panties and frantically waved the wasps away from where minutes before there had been none. I stumbled back along the narrow tunnel of prickly pear cacti, clasping my burning and most intimate part and wondering how to deal with this predicament. What a fine introduction to fieldwork in the Moroccan Rif where there were no mod. cons.: not that I was expecting any, but I was not expecting intimate wasps either, and this despite my first eight years moving around India and my subsequent growing up in Morocco, where my parents decided to live in 1930.

I had longed to travel to the remote and wilder parts of my beloved Morocco—a country which I have always regarded as home—and to face danger. In the early 1930s *any* part of the country south of Marrakesh was considered unsafe and closed to tourism. The French "pacification" of the Berber tribes was under way, and they had cordoned off the area because the Protectorate administration had decreed most of the Atlas mountains and the desert beyond a "Zone of Insecurity." Meanwhile, I had had to make do with fantasies of traveling hard and tough in remote places. Rape, death, or both, at the hand of some armed tribesman would, I fantasized, have been well worth the price.

The Atlas Mountains. . . the Sahara. . . the mountainous Rifian chain east of Tangier were all daydreams of pure magic to me, a teenage girl. How could I know that one day those dreams would become reality when I met David Hart.

"SHIT! KeeRIST! These goddamn doors are made for MIDGETS!" howled an agonized voice. And so Dave thudded into my life. This meeting with Dave—who was to become my husband and introduce me to anthropological fieldwork and the hard and simple life among tribal people, the life I had always longed to lead—had taken place many months earlier in Tangier.

Social anthropology was totally meaningless to me at the time, but Dave was more than happy to instruct an interested listener and, in a nutshell, this is how he explained his discipline:

"A social anthropologist studies a given peoples' laws, social structure, kinship and political systems, notions of justice, religion, morals and ethics, as well as their life crises: birth, marriage, death and any rituals which surround these." He paused, noted my rapt attention and went on: "That means living among the people he studies and speaking their language or dialect."

I nodded, saying, "It's being out in the wilds that interests me, the perfect life! The people and their goats; I don't mind flies or insects; no light, no piped water, no. . ." My voice trailed off as Dave interrupted: "That's just it, that's what gets me!" (I thought he was agreeing with my romantic notions.) "It's what I hate about fieldwork. *No* johns, *no* place to take a crap in comfort." (Dave is American, by the way) "It's either behind a goddamn rock and at the crucial moment a boy minding the goats wanders by, or worse, a group of women strolls past, off to cut grass. . . or it's that fucking cave buzzing with insects. . ."

I was taken aback, for I hadn't heard such strong language in normal conversation, but Dave raced on, quite unaware that he was using "language."

"If it's sunny, it's the flies; if it's raining, my ass gets wet while I huddle over to keep the toilet paper dry. You just can't win."

The flies and such toilet inhibitions did not bother me too much as I pondered the whole question of being in the field among tribal people, learning at least something of their language, Berber, and their customs—in fact, living exactly as they did. That was our first meeting. During a subsequent trip taken with friends to southern Morocco, we had the opportunity to get to know each other better and found that we were both getting very involved emotionally. His family disapproved of our friendship because, technically, I was still married and, furthermore, had three nearly grownup children. Dave often came back from the Rif on some excuse and so we met clandestinely, or so we imagined: but of course everyone knew about it. Shamelessly I did not care; I was madly in love and was going off to lead the life I had always wanted. The line was cast and I was hooked.

It did not matter to me that by then the country of my dreams had changed, and that the interior was no longer "wild" as it had been in the mid-thirties: the Franco-Spanish Protectorate had taken care of that. What did matter was that the chance to travel was just over the horizon. My youthful fantasies came back. I still wanted to see all the corners of "darkest" Morocco, to travel and live among tribesmen, to lead a life of danger perhaps (as I secretly hoped), and definitely one of discomfort. The role that the tribes*women* might play in that life was, oddly enough, something I had not considered at all. That I would spend the major part of my time with *them* hadn't even entered my head. I was prepared to ride mules (or camels) or walk for miles to hamlets where few, if any, Christian women had ever penetrated. So I walked out of my marriage (though not away from my children) and with Dave traveled to many remote places in Morocco, places that in the 1960s were still inaccessible to tourists. With him I was, and still remain, happy and involved in a life that is utterly congenial to us both.

As far as the Rifian women were concerned I was not immediately accepted; they viewed me with suspicion and a certain amount of hostility. I had to learn their language and lifestyle and to get their difficult names right, all of which meant hard work over a long period of time. After many visits the ladies gradually became used to me as one of the family—though with reservations—and let me in on a few of their hopes, their hates and their secrets.

By now, in the 1990s, labor migration to Europe among the men has eased the home economic situation considerably in the Rif, but the wives are usually left behind. So, for the most part, life continues for them as it always has done: a life of seclusion, behind the courtyard door. The following account is of the months of my initiation, because, for the women, few of the customs have changed.

Dramatis Personae

In the Nkur River community of r-'Attaf

Muhand n-'Allush ..... David Hart's assistant and head of household
Arhimu ...... Muhand's mother and head of the women's compound
Mut .... Arhimu's elder sister
Fadhma .... Arhimu's mother
Khadduj .... Muhand's third wife
Yamna and Rwazna .... Muhand's sisters
Dris and Muhammadi ...... Muhand's sons with third wife (Khadduj)
Maghniya .... Muhand's daughter with third wife (Khadduj)
Hmid .... Muhand's son with first wife (Hadduma)
'Aisa n-Bu Tahar .... Yamna's husband
Si 'Abd ar-Rahman .... Rwazna's husband
'Aliya .... the poor, dirty neighbor
Arqiya .... Muhand's niece

In the mountain community of l-'Ass

Bu Tahar Uzarqan ...Muhand's uncle and head of household and family
Fadhma .... Bu Tahar's wife and head of women's compound
Hadduma .... Muhand's first wife
Mimun .... Bu Tahar's eldest son
Fatima .... Mimun's fifteen-year-old wife
Sha'ib w-'Aisa (Chu-Chukth) .... Muhand's half-brother
Dhamimund .... Chu-Chukth's wife
'Allal .... Bu Tahar's second son
'Aisha .... 'Allal's wife (with three children)
Arqiya .. Muhand's fourteen-year-old daughter by second (divorced) wife
Fadhma and Mimuna .... Bu Tahar's teenage daughters
Hammadi n-'Abd al-Qadar ....the bride Arqiya's father-in-law
Arhma .... Hammadi's wife and Arqiya's mother-in-law
Muh .... Arqiya's husband and son of Hammadi
Hadda .... wife of one of Hammadi n-'Abd al-Qadar's sons
Mimuna and Maghniya .... Arqiya's sisters-in-law (both married)
'Ali .... Maghniya's husband

1

New Territory

In 1959, the road from Tangier into the Rif, the northern mountain chain of Morocco, was bad and most of it unpaved. We had driven all day over a rough and twisty trail that climbed up into the mountains, where the magnificent cedar forests of Ketama perfumed the cool air. In a sturdy Land Rover we continued through the lonely countryside and isolated villages to a place called Targuist, a small town of some importance, as this is where, linguistically speaking, the Rif truly begins. It was as though we had stepped through a door. Barren ochre mountains surrounded us, studded with gray boulders on the point of toppling over, while dry gullies split the parched and thirsty earth, an inhospitable land where man and beast worked hard to survive. My heart was captured by this stark and harsh panorama, and it was love at first sight.

We had been traveling for two days and at last were approaching the major mountain market of the Aith Waryaghar tribe, Suq al-Arba‘ Tawrirt: "suq" meaning "market", al-Arba‘ meaning "Wednesday" and "Tawrirt" being an archaic Berber word for "hill" and no longer in current Rifian use. Since it was not market day on that first visit, the place was almost deserted. There is always a resident guardian and a rickety shop or two which remain open for emergency needs such as candles, sugar, tea or matches and the occasional oddball arrivals like ourselves. The market was shaded by mammoth eucalyptus trees, and as we drove in a thin, dusty cat slunk between them, treading delicately and cautiously, glancing from side to side for a possible handout.

It was here that Muhand was to meet us. Muhand was Dave's assistant, top informant and interpreter and they were old friends. Dave had been very much the bachelor when he had left for the United States in the summer of 1955, four years earlier. Muhand, I had learned, was a true macho Rifian who believed that women should keep their place: in the home. So I naturally had qualms about my appearance on the scene. He had been warned of our imminent arrival by telegrams but they could not be relied upon. They would eventually reach the military post and from there messages were delivered on foot and verbally for many miles and in all directions, so communication had to be brief.

We would be spending several months in Muhand's house, which was very remote. It had no modern facilities whatsoever, which was the way I wanted it—or so I thought. But I felt nervous all the same at being the stranger and meeting a crowd of unknown people, the women in particular, to whom I would be a curiosity—for none of them had ever seen a Western woman in Western clothes.

In order not to embarrass Dave or anyone else, I had devised a special fieldworking garb, one that would not be too revealing. Loose blouse, full skirt (or dress) under which I wore a pair of trousers, so that when the constant wind did blow my skirt around or when I sat on the floor my legs would be decently and modestly covered.

To allay my disturbed thoughts, Dave told me something of the people among whom I would be living. Their collective tribal name in their own Rifian language was Aith Waryaghar, the first of many difficult names for me. With "Waryaghar," pronounce the first syllable as in "worry" and the "gh" in the second like a Parisian rolled "r", or the "ch" as in the Scottish "loch." The Aith Waryaghar are the largest and toughest tribal group in the Rif.

As this was a Muslim society Dave had no access to the women whatsoever. So the main thing for me was to adapt myself to the tribeswomen, who were every bit as tough as their men, so that I, too, could do some work among them and, perhaps, gain knowledge of some of their guarded feminine rituals. The "nonthropologist" was being snared into the anthropologist's web!

Muhand's cheerful shout echoed across the compound as he rushed to meet us. Dave tumbled out of the Land Rover and they embraced

Rifian-style, with hugs and much back-slapping thrown in. I stayed in the obscurity of the van and Muhand, with Muslim tact and custom, pretended not to notice me until Dave called out for me to join them, saying, "This is Ursula."

His smile of welcome was all the brighter for two gold teeth, and he clasped and pumped my hand warmly. Fortunately he spoke Spanish, so we had a means of communication which buoyed up my spirits no end. He was a very handsome man dressed, that day, in a striped *jillaba* (a long-sleeved hooded "coat" braided down the front) with European clothes underneath. His turban was immaculately tied and tilted jauntily over the left eye. Muhand was not very tall but he was broad and strong; his eyes, bright as black olives, shone in a square snub-nosed face. He was sizing me up without appearing to do so and I hoped that I stood the test.

Suq al-Arba‘ was at the end of the track. From there to r-‘Attaf, Muhand's tiny hamlet, we had to drive up the partially dry river bed of the Nkur River, one of only two major rivers in the arid central Rif and absolutely impassable after heavy rains. This was the only way to his house, as sheer hills rose from the high banks on either side. Muhand expertly took over the driving, for only he knew how to navigate the treacherous surface. The crust appeared deceptively firm, but a quagmire lurked beneath. The Land Rover tossed and lurched over the smaller boulders like a dinghy in a violent sea.

We traveled in this body-jolting way for about three hours, stopping constantly to give people lifts until there was not an inch of space left. Through the grapevine everyone knew that Dave was returning and had started walking down the river to give him a real welcome. Since we could only crawl along, the retinue had no trouble keeping up with us, joking and laughing and casting furtive glances at me. I did not say a word or even smile. I was not expected to; to all intents and purposes I was invisible.

At long last, as a warning of our approach, raucous blasts on the horn reverberated through the valley. Dave pried a numbed arm free and pointed:

"Look! There is Muhand's house." I craned my neck and peered out through the windshield. On the hill was a low mud house partially surrounded by a thick cactus hedge with some steep trails leading up to it from the river bed. Small children, intent as ants, ran out of the house at the noise of the horn then vanished behind a solid wooden door, no doubt to tell their mother of our imminent arrival. The children appeared again and ran down the path, as sure-footed as goats, to watch our approach. We rocked out of the river bed and stopped where the track ascended abruptly.

"Surely we're not going to *drive* up that?" I was apprehensive as our passengers, along with Dave, spilled out over the trail board. The trail seemed far too steep for even four-wheel drive. I wanted to get out, too, but we had started forward before I could even open the door. My toes curled as we jolted upward and sideways at a crazy angle, slowly inching forward in the lowest of gears, Muhand delighting in his prowess at the wheel and the opportunity to show off. He was a good driver on rough tracks, but once on the paved road he became an irresponsible speed fiend. I clutched at the dashboard as the baggage slid across the floor while thorny cactus scraped the side of the Land Rover, and before I could slide the window shut a prickly pear bounced into my lap, shedding a flurry of microscopic spines over my skirt.

"The joys of the simple life," I reminded myself. With a lurch and a final bass whir of the engine we arrived at the top of the hill and thankfully on to level ground. Muhand turned off the motor, wiped his hands on a rag and turned to me:

"Welcome! Were you nervous?" he asked with a grin, his gold teeth sparkling.

"No, of course not. . . well, a little, perhaps, when the baggage slipped to the side and I wondered if we might tip over."

The others had caught up by now with Dave trailing behind, very much out of breath, as he was not used to striding up hills at the pace of these mountaineers, to say nothing of being out of condition, as I would also find myself to be when tramping around the hills.

"*Arah! Arah!* (Off! Off! Beat it!)," shouted Muhand to the ferocious dogs that were snapping and snarling round us, while I stood there awkwardly feeling self-conscious and conspicuous.

"Well, here you are! What do you think of it?"

The tone was a little too hearty. Dave probably thought that, despite all my assurance that I really liked "primitive" life, maybe the first view of a Rifian house would prove too primitive. Although I did feel like a new girl at school, I was in my element and loving every moment. Dave was all smiles and happiness.

"*This* is where I belong, this is the real Rif; it just blows my mind! And *these* are my boys! Great, aren't they?"

Everyone was shaking hands, backslapping and hugging him. I looked at the "boys" in question: most wore turbans, a few wore squat, round felt fezzes, not at all like the standard fancy dress idea of them. All had the rugged country look; many were barefooted, their feet gnarled and tough, while some wore sneakers with the backs turned down and holes cut out for painful toes. Nearly all were in ragged and torn clothes, though this did not necessarily mean poverty. Sunday, which it was, is just an ordinary working day. Friday is the day of rest and the noonday prayer at the local mosque, although otherwise in the country it was treated pretty much like any other day.

There was a lot of noise, laughter and chattering, with Dave already off telling a joke. I failed to understand a single word and felt very much left out standing there on the edge of the group. I knew they were only being polite by ignoring me, but even so I felt a little resentful toward Dave, unreasonable as I knew it to be. "Childish. . . and a little jealous, perhaps?" an inner voice whispered spitefully.

However, in those few moments I learned a very useful lesson: no matter how much Dave loved me, his work came first, and if I could accept that and live with it, then we would get along fine together.

Muhand, who had gone into the house on our arrival, now appeared through the barn-sized door, followed by two tangle-haired little girls, and shouted to his sons to get started on unpacking the Land Rover. He cuffed his older son across the ear, most unjustly, as he was already busy hauling out the cases. I caught the boy's eye and he gave me a timid smile as if to say, "It's all right, I'm used to it."

The house, along with the others dotted around, all well separated from each other, was just as it had been explained. If elsewhere in Morocco houses may be clustered together to form true villages and protection to the inhabitants, in the Rif they are widely dispersed and are surrounded by thick cactus hedges. This is because the Rifian is suspicious of his neighbors and in particularly jealous fashion guards the seclusion of his women, although any traditonally oriented Muslim never allows his womenfolk to be looked upon by strange male eyes.

In a Rifian community there is no main square, communal fountain or narrow, mud-packed streets. The uninitiated, such as myself, would never know that they were in a "village," as each well-separated house is on high ground so that anyone approaching can be seen. Every dwelling is protected by its own horde of dogs.

It is not anticipating matters to say that, before the year 1921 (which marked the unification of the Rifian tribes under 'Abd al-Krim, and the beginning of his heroic but doomed resistance to the combined colonial armies of Spain and then France until 1926), if there was a blood feud going on between two neighboring families a man felt vulnerable once he had left the safety of his own cactus hedge, which he never did unarmed, as his enemy's gun might be trained upon him. For the blood feud was then the central fact and institution of Rifian political life. However, in the interests of regional unity and the fight against the Christian invader, 'Abd al-Krim abolished the blood feud as well as the little feuding pillboxes which used to stand as redoubts next to each house.

Every Rifian house has its central courtyard, totally secluded, which is the hub of the women's domain, and as we trudged back and forth through this yard with our baggage (the women had been banished), I sensed unseen eyes boring into me from doors opened just a crack and felt clumsy in my Western clothes of combined skirt and trousers.

"Where do we get water?" I asked.

"The women and older girls fetch it from the river, or spring," Muhand replied. "As you will, too," he added teasingly. The spring was a long way off, so they usually went to a spot about a mile down the river where the water trickled moderately clear even though it was never completely free of mud. They also washed their clothes in a parallel channel and laid them out on bushes and stones to dry.

Movement on the other side of the cactus caught my eye and I peered through. There were three most colorfully dressed women, with flamboyant head scarves held in place by twinkling silver jewelry, toiling up the hill with enormous round earthenware jars on their backs that must have weighed a ton.

"Are they part of Muhand's family?" I asked Dave. He glanced quickly over the hedge, then turned away. "I imagine so, though I've only caught glimpses of them as I can never really look. You'll be the one to get to know them." And it was true. Dave, despite considerable time in the Rif, never really knew what the women of Muhand's family looked like as he had to keep well away from them and any other women, too.

I watched them. It was a hard climb up and they walked slowly, never once looking in our direction. "Will I have to carry weights like that?" I murmured to Dave. He smiled as he answered me: "A few days ago I thought I heard you raving about this kind of life with no mod. cons., no piped water, solitude and all kind of jazz. . . You are an incurable romantic, Urse. Fieldwork, as I told you, is hard slogging in uncomfortable conditions with seldom any privacy, combined with attention to detail and meticulous note-taking. That must often be done later sitting cross-legged in a crowded guest room." It was definitely my kind of life and I had no regrets, though my silence was misunderstood.

"You'll be all right," Dave said, giving me a furtive kiss. "The women will treat you for the most part as a guest, and you won't be expected to carry water, but you will have to get used to each other because you will be spending most of your time with them. They will expect it, as will the other men."

A feeling of dismay assailed me for I didn't want to be shut up with the women. I wanted to be with Dave, experiencing what he was experiencing, but I was just being silly again and suffering from a bad attack of shyness.

2

Housework

The conversation was about me, just as though I were an uncomprehending cow in the marketplace. Muhand quite openly looked me over and others covertly glanced my way. Dave forced an occasional laugh and, at times, looked obstinate.

"What are they saying?" As Dave is such a truthful person, I was a little apprehensive. We had agreed—was it only yesterday? How long ago it seemed!—to say we had been married only a few months. Any other situation would have been scandalous and shocking among people who had strict attitudes and mores about women, and whose outlook on propriety concerning them was even straighter than that of the Victorians.

"Don't tell her," was what Muhand must have said, as he sat up quickly from his reclining position on the mattress and shook his head at Dave. There was a silence, all eyes directed at us. The subject was obviously embarrassing, so I let the matter drop. Soon the ritual of tea drinking was over and most of the men disappeared to go home, again warmly shaking Dave's hand while I sat unobtrusively in the background, thankful to be still in Dave's company. When was I going to meet the ladies of the house, I wondered, and hoped that perhaps it might not be until tomorrow. We had the room, briefly, to ourselves.

"Come on Dave," I urged, "what were they saying?"

"Well. . ." Dave hesitated and looked uncomfortable.

"I know!" It was easy to guess. "They think I'm too old for you?" (I am a few years older.)

"Yes. . . but now don't be upset. The general opinion is that I should have married someone about fifteen. A virgin in fact, not a divorcée."

"To us it doesn't really matter, does it? That's what we knew they would think anyway." We laughed and kissed hastily. A thought struck me: "I hope to God you didn't make it worse by telling them that I had a daughter of sixteen?"

"No, but I did say that at least your fertility was assured as you have three children. That went down rather well, I thought," said Dave complacently.

"Really! They'll think I'm an old hag."

"Let's go for a walk and stretch our legs a bit, and I'll show you the general layout of a Rifian house." Scrambling to my feet, I wondered if I would ever get used to sitting for hours with my legs doubled up beneath me.

Rifian houses are usually low and squat, built of mud and stone with flat roofs. The harvest had been brought in and the roof of Muhand's house was most decorative, as it was covered with yellow squash and deep ochre pumpkins the size of church hassocks, while mounds of corn gleamed with the richness and polish of amber beads. The guest room had two entrances. One led directly outside, through which the male guests could come and go freely. Another door opened onto a small hall that led into the central courtyard, the women's part of the house. Off of this were the family quarters, where all the action took place.

The yard was open to the sky. As the rooms had only the tiniest of windows, the family lived mostly in the courtyard unless it was very cold. Branches cut from ancient olive trees formed rafters that jutted from the walls and rested wearily on gnarled, knotted posts. Like the brim of an old straw hat, a fine latticework of bamboo lay across the beams and gave shelter from the rain and protection from the summer heat. The ubiquitous mule was stabled in one corner of the yard, part of which was partitioned off for the goats. The chickens roosted wherever they could find a perch.

At a little distance from the house rose the bread ovens, built of clay and straw and dome-shaped, resembling beehives. Every married woman living under the same roof has her own oven as well as brazier, water and oil jars, and crocks for butter and honey. She also has her own room, possibly two if the house is large, in the privacy of which she and her husband and children eat their evening meal. If unexpected visitors arrive, the men entertain them in the guest room and the women help each other prepare the potluck lunch or dinner. Hospitality is obligatory and of great importance in Islam, and no guest leaves without first having partaken of a meal, however frugal, whatever the time of day or night.

Mint tea drinking in Morocco is both a ceremony and a ritual. When the guest arrives and is comfortably seated, the host shouts through the inner door to the house for one of his sons, or another younger kinsman, to bring in the tea-making accoutrements. The boy places the brass tray with the gracefully shaped metal teapot, sugar box (all of which may be made of silver if the family is well-to-do) and freshly picked mint in front of the guest, or whoever has the highest status if there are several guests present. The burning brazier and kettle are then brought in, and desultory conversation ensues while the tea-maker breaks the sugar cone into lumps with a brass hammer. He measures out the green tea in his cupped palm, drops it into the pot, then stuffs in the mint and sugar. When the kettle is almost boiling, he pours the water into the pot and puts the latter on the brazier to simmer. After a moment he then pours the tea back and forth in his own glass, testing, adding more mint or sugar until it is just to his liking. Then from a height he pours a little tea into each glass, continuing until all the glasses are full. Now the son or host hands them round and each guest murmurs *Bismillah* (In the name of God) as he takes his glass. To show appreciation of the tea-maker's skill everyone slurps his tea noisily.

Three glasses of tea is the observed, required ritual amount, no more, no less, after which, if it is just a passing visit, the guest may leave or get down to business. At big gatherings the tray and paraphernalia are passed from the guest of honor to the next in the pecking order and the ritual is repeated.

"As-Salam 'alaykum" (Peace be upon you), said Muhand behind us, using the polite and standard form of greeting among Muslims. Usually, and much more informally, the salutation of *la bas 'alaykum*, or simply *la bas* (No evil unto you), is employed by Muslims to

members of other faiths and uttered whenever one enters a room or approaches another person, even though one may have been in that room or with that person only ten minutes previously. The return greeting is reversed: *"Wa 'alaykum as-salam"* (And upon you be the Peace). Thus Dave and I replied in unison to Muhand's salutation while his children giggled and scuffed up the dust.

"Say 'How-do-you-do,'" commanded Muhand, sternly pushing the smaller of the two boys forward. They shyly kissed our hands, Dave's first, then mine, for the man is always greeted before a woman and by this hand-kissing act a child shows respect for adults. Muhand held another chubby boy of about eighteen months in his arms.

"Look how Dris has grown!" commented his father proudly. "He is now three and has become nicknamed 'Amirikani' because he is so fair." Indeed he was, with bright yellow curls like any northern European child. Hmid, who had helped with the baggage, was twelve and at the gawky stage. He kicked a stone nervously with a dirt begrimed toe, eyeing me from beneath his brows as he had never seen a Western woman until our arrival. And when I caught his look and smiled at him, he positively squirmed with embarrassment and would have run away had his father not been there.

Muhand tipped his turban right forward and his yes twinkled at me. "Welcome to your home, Oosla. Your husband is a very good friend of mine; I love him with all my heart," he said dramatically, thumping his chest. "We are brothers, and now you are my sister. This house is yours! Go where you like and anything you want is yours too." I thanked him profusely for his warm welcome and generosity, which in his case was sincerely meant.

"Now, we must find a name for you. David is 'Daud.' That is good. But yours, 'Oosla', what kind of a name is that? Nothing!"

I agreed, as I felt that with a name that sounded familiar I would not appear quite so strange to the ladies.

"Tell me some Rifian names as I don't know any," I asked Muhand. He pinched his lower lip and blinked rapidly.

"What about Rwazna?" (pronouned "Roo-az-na").

"Mmm, quite nice... What else?"

"Maghniya?" Muhand raised his eyebrows questioningly.

"What? No, that's too difficult to say." Dave then suggested "Dhamimund," but I didn't like that either. (The "dh" is sounded like the English "th.")

"That's too lispy. I don't feel like a 'Dhamimund.' Tell me some others." Then a timid voice whispered:

"Munat."

The suggestion came from Hmid, who must have guessed what was going on. He cast a frightened glance at his father and then looked hopefully at me. It was a short and easy name and to please him I smiled and nodded my head, and anyway I like it. So I became "Munat."

"That's good; you will soon be *dharifith"* (a Rifian woman) said Muhand turning to Dave. "Now, Bu Jij, I am going to take Munat to meet the women." Hmid snickered.

"Why do you call Dave 'Bu Jij'?" I questioned, innocently repeating the name. Muhand looked embarrassed; his eyes shifted to Dave and stared at nothing in particular. I waited for an answer, curious, never having seen Muhand at a loss. He muttered something about a name one gave to friends and sauntered casually off in the direction of the house.

"Well, what does it mean?"

"It means 'Big Prick,'" replied Dave offhandedly. "Rifians use it jokingly among close friends, rather as you British say 'Old Boy.'"

"But definitely not so stuffy!"

"Munat! My family are waiting for you! They are asking why you haven't been to seen them sooner."

My heart missed a beat. The moment I had been fearing had arrived.

"What do I *say*?" I asked desperately, wishing that Dave could accompany me.

"Just say in Arabic the usual greetings of 'How are you? No evil,'" Dave answered calmly. "They all understand that; it is universal. Don't worry, Muhand will help you and you can speak to them through him. You'll get along fine." And he squeezed my shoulder encouragingly.

The ladies stood in formation in the central courtyard and looked, if possible, more nervous than I at the meeting. The relief at this mutual realization made us all grin simultaneously as we formally greeted and kissed one another. Two kisses on each cheek, alternately, is the correct salutation by the receiving hostesses and the arriving guest. Muhand's mother was about seventy, though she looked much older with the dry, papery skin of the ancient. She held my hand and peered intently into my face. "*La bas*?" she queried. *"La bas! Al-hamdu li-llah!"* (No evil, thank God!), I chanted fervently. She pointed to her eyes and waved her hand in front of them. I thought she meant she was blind and I clucked sympathetically.

"No, she is not blind, but she is losing her sight," explained Muhand. Looking more closely, I saw that there was a film of cataract growing over the pupils and clucked again.

"But don't let that fool you. She is still as agile as a mountain goat on a hillside and as astute as a cat." The old lady's name was Arhimu ("Ar-hee-moo") and she was slender and tiny, no more than four feet eight inches. She was dressed in flowing white muslin—a little gray with age and river washing—plus a white turban headcloth bound round her head. I never saw her without her turban, asleep or awake; and round it she wound the wispy coils of her gray hair. Her expression was gentle and kind as she babbled to me while I smiled and nodded inanely.

"She says," translated Muhand, "that you are as one of the family and this is your part of the house in which to come and go as you like. Do not wait to be invited."

"Baraka llahu fik, baraka llahu fik" (Thank you, thank you, lit. The Blessing of God upon you), I responded, squeezing her hand. We smiled round at each other while Muhand put his hand on a girl's shoulder, saying: "This is Arqiya, my niece. She is going to be married very soon and we will make it a big feast now that you are here." Muhand repeated this in Rifian to a thin, pasty, shy girl who had none of the looks of the other women; just mousy, though she was a mouse with a very warm smile that appealed to me.

Yamna was the name of Muhand's sister. I was very much aware of her piercing black eyes examining every inch of me. She disliked me, I was certain, and would ridicule every faux pas I made once I was no longer considered a guest. Her smile was cold and false but, like her brother, she was very good-looking.

Last to be introduced was Khadduj, who was Muhand's third and youngest wife. She was only fifteen when they had married four years previously, and she had given Muhand three children: Dris ("Amirikani") plus a daughter of two, and finally Muhammadi, the baby. Although Khadduj looked older than her nineteen years, she was very beautiful and blond, as so many Rifians are. Her large, gray eyes, darkened with a sooty finger, were further enhanced and outlined with kohl (powdered antimony), which accentuated the creamy translucence of her skin. Silver jewelry gleamed against her forehead and bangles tinkled on her arms.

Muhand had been married three times. His first wife, to whom he was still married, lived in the old family house some miles away with her five children, of whom Hmid was the eldest. Also living with his first wife was a daughter of a second marriage, a woman he divorced two years later as he suspected her of practicing sorcery on him. Muhand claimed she was working a spell to render him impotent, as she was jealous of Hadduma, the first wife.

La bas, la bas (literally, "No evil?" or "No harm?") was asked and answered ad nauseam until there was an awkward silence and we could only smile at one another.

"Prepare the tea!" ordered Muhand, coming to our aid. The brass kettle was already steaming on the brazier outside the door to his mother's room in which we would drink it, as she was the senior lady of the house, her status being assured by her position as mother-in-law.

Khadduj spread out some matting while her mother-in-law brought forth a tray of glasses, pewter teapot and decorated canisters of tea and sugar. The tray itself had short legs and was more like a portable brass table. As Arhimu squatted and fanned up the charcoal she gave a sharp order to Yamna, who got up slowly and lazily strolled to a room across the courtyard. Taking her time, she finally came back with a chair and dumped it beside the matting where I sat. I could see the going would be tough with her. From previous experience in urban Moroccan homes I knew what was expected of me.

"*Qim dha!*" (Sit there!)" ordered Muhand, pointing to the chair with a short, stubby finger.

"Oh no, Muhand, please! I am quite comfortable here, really!" But as the chair had been specially brought, I had to sit on it feeling stiff and foolish, while my hostesses, in their draped clothes, looked comfortable and elegant sitting on the matting.

Through Muhand translating we chatted of this and that, and his mother told me that once, long ago, she had entertained to lunch the wives of two Spanish army officers. Since then, she said, no other foreign woman had been into the Rifian hinterland. The fact that I was going to be such a curiosity alarmed me. I don't like the limelight.

After we had drunk the customary third glass of tea, Muhand suddenly got up. "Come," he ordered me, feeling perhaps that a little was enough for both sides. "Munat is going back to her husband," he announced to all, and I stood up from my chair while the women rose to their feet in one graceful movement. He expounded further: "She is going to write down and learn Rifian words and phrases so that you women can talk together." Relieved, we nodded and smiled politely and clasped hands and patted each other's backs. Then I followed Muhand to the guest room and the men's part of the house.

I felt sorely in need of a drink—a surreptitious one, of course—and was most put out when I went to our cache of the "emergency" bottle only to find the larder bare. Someone had been even more surreptitious than I!

Except for standard greetings, the Moroccan Arabic I had learned as a child in Tangier was of no use among the women, who were tribal and monolingual, speaking only Berber. Filching some of Dave's note cards, I cut them, much to his annoyance, into small squares. With Muhand's help I spent the remainder of the evening writing down current household words and useful sentences with the corresponding English or Spanish on the reverse side. I carried these with me constantly in a bag and at odd moments I would fumble for a small square, look at one side, and try to come up with the word on the reverse. The word/phrase bank increased as did my vocabulary, which I practiced on anyone prepared to listen. At night in my dreams words were shouting at me, louder, louder. . . Then there *was* somebody shouting; the dream became reality.

"Get up! Get up! We have to spring clean today."

The guest room was our bedroom at night, sometimes shared by stayers-on whereupon I would be allocated a place to sleep in Arhimu's room. We sat up on our respective, narrow mattresses and looked out of the window. It was barely daylight, yet the household already sounded busy. Scarcely had we finished dressing when the door flew open and Muhand burst in, full of energy, carrying a tray.

"Sbah l-khayr!" Good morning! *La bas!* Slept well?" He did not wait for our reply: "Hmid! HMID! Here, bring some glasses, you fool!" Muhand shook his head irritably. "He's an idiot, that boy; he is only fit to be a donkey. No better than his mother in fact." (The wife of the first marriage.) Hmid, however, was not in the least simple-minded. He had a hearing defect which made him speak rather oddly, so he was shy and stammered; therefore his father thought him stupid. The poor kid could never do things right.

We were not allowed to linger over coffee. Muhand was hustling Dave from the room with orders to his son to take him off to a neighbor's house to sit in *his* guest room. Dave grumbled and muttered as I bundled our clothes back into the suitcase.

"Muhand, wait! I need my briefcase. . . ink! Perhaps the cameras too. Urs! Where're the cameras?" "Hanging from that nail in front of you, in full view!" Dave rushed about distractedly assembling the things he needed for what might be an entire day's absence.

"It's always the same," he remarked. "They keep you waiting for days, often don't even show up, yet when *they* want to get something done they can't even wait five minutes. Haven't even had time to go to the cave for a crap behind the cactus. . . goddamn it!" Dave practically decapitated himself slapping at a fly using his bald head for landing practice. It was a mystery how he didn't suffer violent headaches from the blows he gave himself.

All our things had been whisked outside and I dived after the disappearing carton containing the rolls of toilet paper. "You had better put this in your briefcase," I called, throwing over a roll. As Dave and Muhand left I wished I did not have to be left entirely alone to cope so early on in the game of adjusting. However, that was what it was all about, and I had my bag of words and sentences.

"I've decided Hmid will stay here," said Muhand. "He'll show you what do to; I've told him to look after you. . . And you've got to learn sometime," he added as an afterthought. No sooner had the outer door shut than the women flocked in from the courtyard.

"La bas! La bas! La bas!" we chorused to each other and, without further ado, we got to work to haul the double brass bedstead from where it was tightly wedged at the end of the room. Squeezing myself among them I also set to, to help pull and lift it out.

The nuptial bed is a status symbol. Seldom is it used except for sitting upon on occasions such as a baby's name-giving or a small boy's circumcision feast. Then it is the women's turn to use the guest room. This particular bed was half hidden by bright pink satin-frilled curtains with a spread to match without a crease in it. The other mattresses along the floor were upholstered in vivid flowered cotton, while a width of the same material lined the walls behind the divans.

As we hauled the furniture outside I tried out some of the words and phrases I had learned. This rather delayed proceedings as the ladies hadn't a clue what I was trying to say and they politely stopped work to listen. They never laughed because they did not recognize it as their own language and assumed I was talking to them in mine. It was Hmid who suddenly realized I was making tottering steps in Rifian. He didn't laugh either, probably because his own stuttering made him aware and sympathetic toward the conversational efforts of others.

The room was now completely bare and ready for the walls to be whitewashed. Arhimu had prepared the wash (from rocks of lime) as a thick paste to be spread on by hand as Rifian women do not use brushes to do this work. Khadduj showed me how I should smooth it on in a circular motion, but the lime so stung and burned my hands that I stopped after a while. Yamna laughed sarcastically, shrugged her shoulder at me for being so useless and then turned and continued her work. I smiled apologetically, feeling guilty for such a tender skin. "I want to learn", I faltered as Khadduj understandingly nodded her head. She was kind, and though we could scarcely converse, we got along. Muhand's mother came to the rescue and found something to keep me busy. She gave me a stick and indicated I was to keep stirring a mud-colored liquid in a bucket. Hmid was my constant companion, pointing out objects and telling me their names and making signs for me to write them down.

Apart from stirring what I learned was a clay and lime concoction, I sat with the children and made rough brushes from small fir branches, tying them together with strips of palmetto leaf. Then with these branches we smeared the mixture over the floor and left it to dry.

In the interim, we took a walk along a culvert to collect leafy lentiscus twigs. The lentiscus is a small but tough drought-resistant bush that grows profusely throughout the circum-Mediterranean belt, including North Africa. We took the great armfuls we had collected back to the house, and, with big stones, the children started to pound and bruise our bundles. The broken leaves that fell off were put into a zinc tub and left to soak. The berries, too, are used for a variety of purposes: cosmetics, dyes and a substance for floor polish.

Now it was time to have a break for tea and a snack of highly-spiced lentils with plenty of bread to dunk in the oil. The olive oil was homemade and very rich and pungent and I tried, unsuccessfully, to dive the piece of bread beneath it to get at the sauce and lentils. The ladies lolled about and dawdled over tea and listened patiently while I repeated the words I had learned that morning. They responded with signs and pantomine by asking me equally simple questions. However, we were not allowed to loaf for long. Arhimu bustled up, clapped her hands and got all of us to our feet.

"Work! Work! The men will be returning soon and there is still the bread to bake." Or this is what I supposed she said, as I caught key words for "work," "man" and "bread." Arhimu took my arm and pointed to the bucket of lentiscus "lotion" and then to the guest room where I was to take it. Arqiya and I sloshed the mixture over the clay-and cement floor while Khadduj and Yamna worked it in with sacking. Since Rifian women do this task several times a year, over the course of time the floors acquire a lustre that any Western housewife would be proud of.

One trait I had observed in Arab women and noted to be the same with Rifian ones is that, when they do jobs that require bending down, they do not crouch forward with bent knees as we do. They lean forward with their knees straight, their bottoms go up in the air while their spines seem to dip in the middle as they swing their arms and shoulders rhythmically from the waist. Excellent for the figure. I tried emulating this posture and movement myself, but my spine only arched and refused to dip provocatively. My companions shrieked with laughter at these attempts to copy them.

The spring cleaning was finished and the room was clean, blank and expressionless. Hurriedly we restored its character by tacking the cretonnes back into place, fought the bed into its position in the alcove and rearranged the mattresses. All was spic and span for the coming wedding and the expected guests. And Muhand's mother had not been idle; she had cleaned up the courtyard and tidied away the unsightly pots and other household clutter, for it was in the yard that the dancing would take place.

As I sat with the women in Arhimu's room waiting to share whatever the men left us of the vegetable stew *(tajin)* the atmosphere was relaxed. Arqiya repaired a drum for the coming festivities and Yamna, using my stiff hair brush, pulled it sensuously through her long, black hair. I was happy to be ignored and to listen to the sound of their words as they chattered unselfconsciously around me.

3

Getting to Know Them; Sacrifice of the Fatted Calf

"Umm?" Sleepily I tried to shrug off the hand shaking my shoulder.

"Come on, Urse, you've got to get up. The men want to come in."

"It's only dawn! I want to sleep a bit longer," I protested, and turned over, fooling myself that I could do so as I was a guest. There was a knock and the tray of glasses rattled outside the door. We both sighed resignedly and dressed as fast as possible.

Later, armed with notebook and cards and accompanied by a sleepy Hmid, I went to join the ladies in the courtyard. There was still some coffee left so Yamna handed me a glass and actually smiled. Despite the early hour, everyone was busy with food preparations. Muhand was about to slaughter a large rabbit, and before I could escape from witnessing the killing he slit its throat.

According to Muslim dogma and ritual, all meat for human consumption is sacrificed by the male head of the household. As he severs the jugular vein of the animal or fowl, he utters the sacrificial phrase *"Bismillah Allahu Akbar"* (In the name of God, God is most Great). A sacrifice is not considered to be properly performed if the sacrificer saws at the animal's throat. It must be done with one clean sweep of the knife. After that the women take over.

Now Khadduj had slit the skin and worked it off the rabbit with the help of her little daughter. When young girls are little more than toddlers, they start to learn the rudiments of housekeeping and caring for younger members of the family. As they grow older their responsibilities increase, so that by the time they are ready for marriage they are competent housewives.

The rabbit's steaming entrails were removed and with Maghniya ("Ma-ran-ee-a") holding the slimy mess in her pudgy, baby hands, her mother started to unravel the intestines as though they were yards of wool. Everyone from Granny Arhimu to Dris watched all this in eager anticipation. They insisted that I, too, squeeze the warm and slippery innards, since they assumed I could distinguish between a healthy rabbit and a sick one. It was all a little too raw for so early in the morning. Arqiya pegged the skin onto a circular frame and put it close to the brazier. As soon as it had dried, she shaved off the fur and handed the nude skin to me. What was I supposed to do with it? Muhand, who was in and out, paused in his own work to help me in my dilemma.

"Munat, Arqiya wants you to help by rubbing salt into the skin and kneading it with your fingers to keep it supple. We can make a new tambourine with that skin, or keep it for repairing a broken one. Rabbit skins don't make the highest quality tambourines, but they are good enough for children to learn on. . . and you too!"

Muhand threw back his head and laughed. Grabbing an old tambourine that hung from a nail in the wall, he gave it a few masterly strokes that reverberated round the yard. My heart lifted with excitement. This was the life I had imagined: stars and drums, and a handsome drummer straight out of "The Desert Song"—a fantasy not shared by my academic husband!

There was work to do and the men were almost as busy as the women. As he went outside, Muhand threw the drum to Hmid. I wanted to have a try. "Me," I said, tapping my chest and reaching out to take it from him. Confidently, and with my fingers spread across the skin, I flourished the other hand as I had seen Muhand do. "Blap, blap, blap" was the dead, flat sound I produced. The echoing rhythm that should have been there was missing. Dris and Maghniya squealed with laughter, while Khadduj smiled tolerantly, as she would to a child. Hmid giggled and took the drum back again. With a few deft twists of his hand, he brought forth rhythmic throbs. His brown eyes sparkled mischievously and his tongue stuck out from the corner of his mouth in concentration.

I learned that the good tambourines are made from sheep or goat skins and require a lot of patient work. The thin wooden frame has to be soaked for several days in water to mold it into its circular form. Muhand, who had disappeared into his room, brought out his own tambourine. It was beautifully decorated: across the inside center of the skin were two fine strands of wool on which minute beads had been threaded to give resonance, while the outside had been painstakingly decorated with geometrical designs and dots.

"This is lovely! Who made those intricate patterns?"

"Khadduj made this," replied Muhand, turning the drum over in his hands. "Each woman makes her own, and often one or two more to spare, if she has the time and the skin isn't needed for anything else. And we don't lend them out to any odd drummer either," he added sternly.

I smiled my appreciation to Khudduj, who shrugged her shoulders modestly, but her expressive gray eyes were alight with pleasure and just pride.

At that moment the hum of men's voices mingled with the bleating of a goat and a ferocious barking announced that people were arriving. Just then a very pretty and plump woman walked in, gay and self-possessed.

"As-Salam 'alaykum!" (Peace be upon you), she called out cheerfully to all present, and was in turn greeted affectionately with much hugging and kissing, chatter and laughter. She received a special welcome from Arhimu, I noticed. She looked at me curiously and Arhimu drew me into the circle. She was Muhand's youngest sister and Arhimu's favorite daughter, Rwazna. Muhand called this information to me as he stuck his head round the door.

"Come outside, we are going to kill the goat. All the relatives are here; they are all old friends of Bu Jij." The women tittered as they went off to watch the fun and I made as if to follow, then slipped off to the guest room for a few moments of quiet, if possible with Dave. Luckily, he was alone. "Are you going to watch the fun?" I asked, but Dave shook his head, saying that he had seen it all before many times and noted it all down along with photos. It would be better to stay out of the way as the women, accompanied by their men, were beginning to arrive.

I personally did not relish the spectacle of an animal the size of a goat being slaughtered with blood spurting everywhere, but I could not shame Dave by staying away or shirking whatever woman's task I could help in. Even so, I was determined to have a brief respite first. I plopped down on the mattress, stretching out my legs and leaning back against the wall, feeling deliciously decadent. In Moroccan Muslim society it is not considered polite or decent to stick one's feet straight out, as they should always be tucked decorously beneath one's garments. Dave smiled across at me as I indulged myself in this position and brazenly lit a cigarette. The men would have had a fit had they seen me, even Muhand.

"How are you getting on? Not too much of a strain?" Dave actually looked concerned—worried, perhaps, that I was disillusioned in the everyday realities of fieldwork. He need not have worried. It was a strain, of course, especially the language barrier. But I was making progress in talking *at* the women who were getting to understand me, although I still had trouble understanding *them*. Dave grunted, as he had been through it all before himself—and when he was a green new arrival from America, too.

"Hmid is a marvel," I commented, "guessing at what it is I want to communicate, and getting their replies across to me. He's such a kind little boy, so comprehending for his age. Yet, except for his granny, everyone seems against him." Dave seemed more concerned about the awful, stinging flies.

"Goddamn them! Fucking flies! How I hate all MFI's!"

"MFI's? What are they?. . . and don't use such language!"

"Mother-fucking-insects!" And Dave gave another slap at his head. "However, whether you're getting by with the language or not, tread carefully. Try to be impartial," he cautioned. "Don't take sides; be an *observer*." How very smug, I thought, and smiled to myself. Outward impartiality and non-involvement would be very difficult in that small, narrow, closeknit feminine world.

The pace had been so fast and busy since our arrival, the guest room always full of people, that Dave and I had scarcely had time either to compare notes or talk quietly together. When bedtime came, I was both mentally and emotionally exhausted. Now there was a pause in which I felt I could voice a worry that had been nagging at me.

"I get along fine with the women. Muhand's mother understands that Western ways are different. Through you, and what Muhand himself has learnt from you and passed on, I am adapting myself to their ways." I hastened to add: "Khadduj and Arqiya seem to accept me almost as they would a puppy that had been foisted on them and has to be taught. But I just can't make any headway with Yamna. She seems against me no matter what I do."

Yamna was evidently a family thorn, and Dave was unconcerned.

"Don't let that worry you. You're not the only person she refuses to get on with. Muhand has told me several times that she has been a family problem for a long time and that she's a bitch. No matter where she is, she revels in stirring up trouble. She has been married but couldn't get along with her in-laws. She hasn't actually been repudiated, but it will probably come to that. According to Muhand," Dave added, "she is discontented with her lot as a Rifian woman. Her husband has worked in France and she has heard him telling Muhand about our ways of life and the freedom of Western women with none of the hard work, such as fetching water, cutting grass or milling barley. Now she is pestering him to take her to France. Of course no Rifian wants *his* woman to have that kind of freedom, and anyway, they think every Western woman is a whore. Muhand is quite convinced about that."

"That helps me to understand her better. She is probably even resentful of the fact that I am free to move between the courtyard and the guest room. I must make a special effort with her—give her some European make-up and something. Whatever the difficulties or patience required, I love it here, I love your job. . ."

"It's not a 'job,' it's a *profession*, a *discipline,*" Dave interrupted indignantly—and to think that not so long ago I had never heard of social anthropology!

Further conversation was brought to an end by Si 'Abd ar-Rahman barging in. With a sigh we exchanged resigned looks and struggled to our feet. Dave introduced us. Si 'Abd ar-Rahman was Muhand's brother-in-law, Rwazna's husband. He was tall and slim with gentle, thoughtful hazel eyes. Like Muhand, he too wore Western clothes beneath his *jillaba,* with his turban tipped at a rakish angle over an eyebrow.

"You don't want to be in here all by yourselves!" he exclaimed. "Muhand has sent me to fetch you. The goat is skinned, but he has bought a calf for the occasion and we're just getting ready to sacrifice it. Come and watch." He turned to Dave, adding: "You come along, too, as the women are inside cutting up the goat." Si 'Abd ar-Rahman walked ahead of us out of the room and we followed reluctantly. Muhand's feelings would have been hurt if we had not gone to watch the event, as it is not often that something as expensive as a calf is killed for a wedding in the Rif. He was really making this a special occasion for us; the least we could do was to be appreciative. Stepping through the auxiliary front door we walked round to the open ground in front of the main entrance.

"La bas 'alaykum!" (How are you!), we called as we approached a group of busy men who cheerfully chorused back the response. Muhand resharpened the already sharp knife and rolled up his shirt sleeves. Two men grabbed the calf, one pulling its head back, then intoning *"Bismillah Allahu Akbar."* Muhand slit the calf's throat from ear to ear in one movement. It was so swift that the calf did not even moo. I relaxed; the sacrifice was not half as bad as I had imagined it. The blood did not spurt out in a fountain but just pumped forth powerfully. The kids splashed some of it on the front door and over the threshold to bring luck and prosperity.

Scattering the children, a very spry, gnome-like man came running out of the door with a kettle of steaming water. His eyes were green and merry and his clothes ragged, while an equally ragged piece of cloth that served as a turban bobbed precariously on the back of his head. Not waiting for an introduction, he grabbed my hand in his two coarse work-grimed ones and smiled at me engagingly as he shook it. He was Muhand's maternal half-brother, Sha'ib w-'Aisa, nick-named "Chu-Chukth" because, as a small boy, his way of attracting attention had been by saying "chu-chukth" and clucking like an aggrieved hen.

Chu-Chukth spoke a little Spanish and some Arabic, so we were able to converse. As he hurried over to the spasmodically kicking calf, I asked him what he was going to use the water for. "One moment," he said, "then I'll explain." Curious, and a little sickened, I watched as Chu-Chukth poured water into the calf's ear. "You see," he continued matter-of-factly, "doing this takes the pain of dying away quickly, as a calf does not die the way a goat or a sheep does—a few kicks and that's it."

He went on explaining over his shoulder as he added more hot water to the kettle: "You keep pouring in a gentle stream, a little hotter and still hotter, so the animal's brain just fades away—like an engine failing." Chu-Chukth groaned a "wa-wa-waaa" sound and his voice grated low as he imitated the last whir of a dying battery. What he said seemed true: the water did appear to have the effect of an anesthetic as the calf now lay unconscious on the ground, the blood pumping out weakly till it pumped no more. The animal was dead.

Having performed the sacrifice, Muhand considered that his work was over, and he now reclined indolently on some matting against the wall of his house. Tilling land, sowing, picking olives and the rest of the agricultural cycle of work he regarded as too menial for himself, and he relegated these tasks to others. Being his late father's only son, with a widowed mother, he was the head of the family. As such, he felt that his job was to command, which could best be done from a sitting position. Squatting in a sunny corner chain-smoking, Muhand directed operations. His younger kinsmen rushed about and even his mother was on the run, back and forth, so I tagged on to her and helped fetch basins in which to carry the intestines and offal. Dave, festooned with cameras, was photographing each stage of the operation from every angle.

One man with a thin pointed knife cut small slits into the calf's fetlocks and belly. Chu-chukth and another man inserted sharp, hollowed-out bamboo sticks into these slits and began to flow air under the skin, while Arhimu and Hmid loosened the hide from the still-warm flesh.

"Go and help, Munat," ordered Muhand, "you are a Rifian woman now," and he threw over a stout stick. Confidently I joined in. It looked so easy, but it was not long before I flagged. I kept changing the stick from one hand to the other, I was out of breath, my hair got into my eyes. Meanwhile, Arhimu, old and half blind as she was, kept going untiringly, with strong, evenly-paced strokes. Hmid grinned, pinched his well-developed biceps and pointed to my arms, shaking his head. I agreed with an exhausted sigh, for no muscle bulged in my arms, which were without strength. What a useless, ineffectual being I was. Yamna should have been there to see for herself that a Western woman could not even do a task that was left to the old or to children.

The smaller children were noisy and excited and kept running hither and thither, while the dogs, hoping for a handout more substantial than a crust or chicken bones, yapped expectantly and were kept at bay by well-aimed stones. The anticipation of the coming feast lent a zest to our task, and had this been a Western, non-Muslim household, corks would have been popping and glasses tinkling.

I could have done with some alcoholic stimulant to offset the cloying smell of blood and meat freshly slaughtered. The gory hide had been draped over the hood of the Land Rover and Chu-Chukth was busily scrubbing it clean. It was he, I noticed, who did all the really messy jobs, such as butchering the carcass, having previously humped it into the courtyard on his back. No wonder he had not bothered to dress up!

Dave had gone back into the house as more and more women were arriving. Their menfolk, meanwhile, trooped into the guest room. I hung around outside, hesitating, not knowing quite what to do. I was reluctant to join the gabble of feminine voices which mentioned my name several times in tones that sounded curious, amused or mocking. *I* was the big topic of conversation, and I preferred to remain invisible. I could hear the questions, subdued giggles and more comments. Dare I join the men? That would probably be considered brazen, since a woman's place is behind the courtyard door.

"Damn David," I thought. (It was "David," not "Dave," when I was annoyed.) "There he is gossiping and joking with his cronies and forgetting all about *me*." I stared moodily at the cactus hedge, feeling out of place. A hand tugged at mine, and there was Hmid staring at me, perplexed, yet sensing that I was upset. He smiled, picked up a stone and tapped it, saying *"Azru, azru,"* the Berber for "stone," while making writing motions. So I fumbled for the notebook and dutifully wrote down the word, sulking. This childish behavior was quite unwarranted, as Hmid had been sent to fetch me to the guest room. I had not been forgotten after all.

I. Photographs taken at the Lower House
in the Nkur River community of r-'Attaf

Looking up toward Muhand's house

View over the valley from the cave lavatory

Close-up of Muhand's house, surrounded by prickly pear cactus

Inside the courtyard of Muhand's house

Muhand on a cold day

Khadduj, Muhand's third wife

Dhamimund, Rwazna and Arhimu

Arhimu,
Muhand's mother

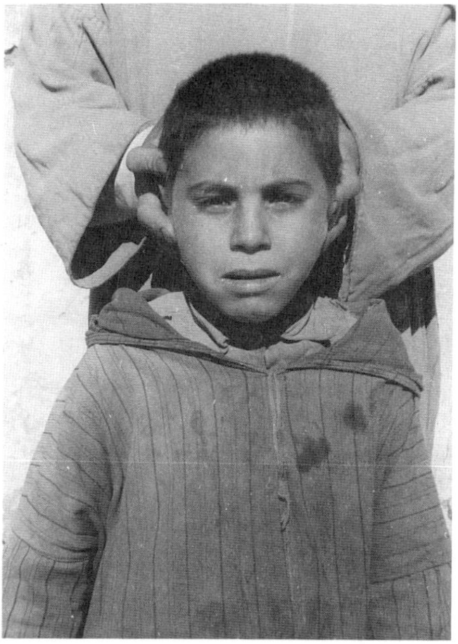

Ill-treated Hmid, with his head being squeezed

Dris (“l‘Amirikani”)

The author with Muhand and two of his children

4

The Wedding Walk . . . and Not a Thing to Wear

When we set off originally, I never expected to have the good luck to attend a wedding. Weddings are, after all, one of the major occasions for festivity in the community and, in the Rif, they consist of three days of celebrations, music and dancing.

Muhand, the bride's uncle, a natural host and master of ceremonies, was to be responsible for the arrangements, and was determined that his niece's marriage would be one Rifian wedding that we would always remember. Because her father was dead, Muhand had taken over her welfare and, as his final responsibility, he had arranged a good marriage for her.

No expense was spared. As noted, a goat and a truly fatted calf were killed, and despite the considerable outlay involved, Muhand refused all financial offers from Dave. The bride was going to a very strict and sober family who belonged to a religious order (the Darqawa) which prohibited its members from dancing, singing or making music unless for religious purposes. (It also maintains, uniquely among Muslim orders in Morocco, a taboo on coffee-drinking.) It seemed to me arguable that the match was such a good one. Muhand well knew what life would probably be like for his niece in these austere surroundings, and he was determined that the marriage would be a magnificent affair, in order to give his niece, Arqiya, a really cheerful send-off.

"Say no more!" said Muhand, as he vigorously shook our hands. "This will also be *my* party of welcome to you both."

The custom is for the groom's family to take charge of all food and entertainment throughout the three days of festivities. In addition, the father of the groom, or his closest relative, traditionally pays the bride's father an agreed sum of money for the girl's hand (bride-price or *sdaq*). The amount depends on the wealth of the family concerned, both in tribal and urban areas. With part of this bridewealth, the father buys his daughter her jewelry and trousseau. These become her exclusive property and cannot be taken away from her should she be divorced—a moderately common occurrence. The most usual reason for divorce is that the wife is barren or unable to produce sons; either way this calamity is always the wife's fault. But almost as common is a wife's alleged bad temper, especially if she cannot get along with the other women in the household. The ideal young bride should always be submissive to her in-laws and a hard worker. Her status begins to improve considerably once she has a few sons to show off, and she is at her peak in the household when she becomes a mother-in-law herself.

Qur'anic law allows Muslims to have four wives at a time, but today, for economic reasons, they seldom have more than one. If they do, each wife must have her own home, or separate quarters, and the husband is supposed to divide his time fairly between them and to treat them all equally as far as clothes and presents are concerned. This is the ideal, but not necessarily the reality.

For the girl's first marriage, it is vital that she bears sons, for they will inherit their father's land and help till and look after it. Prior to 1920, when bloodfeuds were the order of the day in the Rif, many sons provided extra strength and firepower that successfully defended any family and its patrimony. In the case of a divorce, whatever the cause, any children over the age of two (the age at which they are usually weaned) stay with their father and are cared for by his new wife, his mother, or one of his brother's wives.

A bride must be a virgin, for if she is discovered not to be so at marriage, the whole of her bridewealth is returned to the cheated husband's family. The girl is then immediately divorced, and may even be killed to wipe out the stain she has put on the family honor. Today in rural areas such customs can sometimes be circumvented and honor maintained through "arrangement," but in remote tribal regions a girl off on her own somewhere would immediately be viewed with suspicion and disapproval. Adultery is rare, since it, too, used to be avenged by death for both parties, unless they could escape to another tribe. Although in modern Morocco the government takes a dim view of such vengeance, it can still happen. At the very least, those involved can expect total ostracism. For a man without a tribe is a man with no roots and therefore a man without honor—a man who, viewed traditionally, is socially dead.

As far as Muhand's niece was concerned, however, these possibilities never entered her head. She was a model of propriety and convention, and in keeping with convention there was the excitement of her marriage to look forward to. The first two nights of celebrations would take place at separate parties in the houses of both bride and groom. Since we were guests of the bride's family, it was with them that we spent these two evenings. For these first two nights outsiders are never as a rule invited by either family, so it was a great honor to be included in such a personal family affair.

On the third night, prior to the bride's leaving for her husband's home the following day, everyone in the area is welcome, and these are the festivities that are remembered. The formalities involved in the marriage have already been taken care of by meeting with the local *qadi* (a man somewhat similar to a magistrate, versed in Qur'anic law). In his presence a contract is signed laying out the conditions— mainly financial—under which the marriage is to take place, and the girl formally expresses her consent. Now comes the time for that dry formality to be given some life and joy, and it is to this that the third night of the wedding celebration is directed—although I wonder if the real pleasure is not confined to the guests, as the bride and groom spend their time in a series of elaborate rituals!

The groom, himself, sits on a carpet wearing a white *jillaba* with his face completely covered by the hood to symbolize that he, too, is a virgin like his bride (if it is a first marriage). As the guests arrive, they are expected to throw money into his lap to offset the expenses of the wedding. The actual sum donated does not matter, for poverty in the Rif used to be the rule rather than the exception. (This has changed considerably in recent years with the migration of many Rifian workers to Europe.) So nobody felt ashamed if he could give only a small amount; it was, after all, the symbolism that counted. For the bride, Arqiya, there was no present-giving at all. Her close friends had given her trinkets, possibly a dress, and her maternal relatives a little money. But there was no ceremony made of it as in urban weddings, where a woman with a strong voice called out the name of every donor and a description of the gift.

This wedding presented me with a problem. In the Rif the bride traditionally wears her oldest clothes until she goes to her husband's house and the marriage is consummated. Arqiya was swathed like a cocoon in white muslin over a very old shift. Unfortunately the same tradition does not extend to the guests, and I had come completely unprepared. The other women were already clad in their finery and gathered round expectantly to see what I would offer in the way of sartorial splendor. Reticence has never played a part in Rifian life, so ignoring their stares and probing fingers I rummaged in the suitcase knowing full well that I had nothing appropriate for such an occasion. I cursed my lack of foresight and remembered with irritation Dave's vagueness about suitable clothes. He, after all, was supposed to be the expert on local custom, but it never crossed his mind to warn me to bring a festive skirt and a few strings of beads. Nor, in all fairness, had the possibility of a wedding (or a circumcision) occurred to me.

With a sigh I shoved the suitcase in a corner and went in search of Dave for advice, not really expecting that he would have anything useful to suggest. Nor was I disappointed, for he did not really understand this essentially feminine problem and looked up from his notes with an irritated frown. I turned away, realizing that whatever solution was found would have to be one that I worked out with the help of the ladies. They, of course, looked quite stunning in their long, billowing kaftans of richly embroidered brocades. Superimposed over this already exotic attire floated a *dfina,* a diaphanous over-dress embroidered with gold thread or colored silks. They wore bright chokers of tiny beads along with pearls, while the married women had added chains of silver coins and their foreheads gleamed with yet more rows of silver medallions; the richer the husband, the more profuse the gold and silver jewelry. Also, the married women covered their heads in silk scarves of brilliant basic colors on a black background. Single girls tied their hair back with a simple cotton scarf, kept in place by an *aharraz*, a stiff, broad band of material similar to a tiara rising higher in front and worn straight across the forehead. These vivid crowns scintillated with multicolored sequins and braid.

The courtyard echoed with the chatter and shrill laughter of women who had not seen each other for some time and who had plenty to discuss and gossip about. Young married women just do not go visiting, so they only see one another at festive occasions and, occasionally, deaths. Sometimes at births, too, but that depends on how close the relationship is.

"La bas 'alayk, Munat, come over here and sit down." It was Arhimu. A hush fell over the courtyard and every eye was riveted on me as I walked across to her. A thin, angular woman detached herself from an elderly circle of people and came up to me; she was dressed in white, with large safety pins at crucial points holding her clothes together.

"I am Mut, Arhimu's sister. All well with you, *la bas?*" I replied, "All well, thanks be to God!"

"La bas," I said again as we joined the group of women consisting of Muhand's mother-in-law and other relatives, as well as maternal and paternal aunts. With surprise I saw that among this group was a very frail woman propped up by cushions. Her limbs trembled with age and her skin, which was puckered with a million wrinkles, was white and translucent as though it had not seen the light of day for many a year. She stretched out her scaly hand in my direction, so I held it. She could not possibly have just arrived, so she must have been living in the house all the time without my knowing it.

"La bas 'alayk?" I murmured and gently patted her shoulder. Her watery, faded eyes stared vaguely and sightlessly past me. "Who are you?" she demanded in a surprisingly strong voice.

"Munat," I replied, "the wife of the Amirikani," but she didn't hear me, or didn't understand.

"This is my mother," said Arhimu. "She is one hundred and two years old and is still in good health. . . *al-hamdu li-llah!"* Then she bent down and started a long monologue in her mother's ear about who I was. This ancient lady nodded from time to time, and her furrowed, sunken lips twitched in an effort to smile. She still had hold of my hand as I squatted there, while another crinkled claw crept out from the folds of a garment almost as old as the woman herself, and felt up my arm. Bony, crooked fingers examined the contours of my face while everyone silently watched this groping inspection. Even the younger women had paused in their gossiping as though aware that judgment was about to be passed. Suddenly the old woman pulled my face down to hers and planted a dribbly kiss on my cheek that seemed to last forever. Finally she released me and I sat back, inwardly repelled while manners prevented me from wiping that wet kiss from my skin.

"She likes you!" breathed old Arhimu about her senescent mother, which I took to mean that if the old matriarch accepted me, so would the others. I was handed some tea and we sipped in silence, Arhimu being busy with her duties as hostess and head of the household. The older matrons were content just to scrutinize me. I bandied about a word or two, but they assumed that any attempts at conversation would be wasted effort. How handsome Yamna looked, I thought, as I sipped the tea, and how well green set off her flashing eyes. I felt like a dowdy bird with no gay plumage, but was glad to be sitting among these quiet ladies who were dressed in their everyday clothes and among whom I felt gratefully inconspicuous and hoped I could remain that way.

All at once there was a bustle in the yard as young girls jostled each other to warm the skins of their tambourines over the braziers and tentatively test them for resonance, then tried on and swapped sun glasses with one another. They were twittering in excitement and kept glancing across at me. Arqiya came over and grabbed my arm and pulled me to my feet and over to her circle. We clustered chattering around the door and Arqiya made walking movements with her fingers, pointing out to the hills. To accompany them on a walk? I queried by signs. What fun to go with them, I nodded. Khadduj had other ideas. "No." She shook her head firmly. I had to assert myself.

"Yes," I nodded equally firmly. This was followed by a torrent of words from Khadduj, and Hmid was sent scurrying off to the guest room for help and interpretation. He was back in a moment with his father.

"What's the matter?" asked Muhand, and before I could answer, Arqiya plunged in with a flood of explanations and some obvious wheedling. Muhand looked doubtful.

"The girls want you to accompany them, so we must ask David." Again Hmid was sent off to the guest room.

"Dave is not going to mind," I remarked. I didn't need his permission for such a trivial thing.

"Even so, his permission must be asked," insisted Muhand sternly.

"Of course!" I must suppress that Western habit of freedom of action and making my own decisions. Muhand came panting back nodding affirmatively, his eyes shining.

"Right, you may go on the wedding walk!" announced Muhand, as though the permission came from him. He then proceeded to give me his explanation of the "wedding walk."

Everyone knows about the forthcoming marriage, but it is customary for the bride and her maids of honor to visit every house and family who live rather far away to issue invitations to all the single girls. They are expecting her, and it is then that they give her their presents. Muhand looked at me dubiously, as it was a strenuous walk that would take all day, but I wasn't concerned about that.

However, a thought struck me: apart from my looking odd, they might feel embarrassed having me along. It was not customary for a married woman to leave the confines of her small world.

"Of course not!" Muhand encouraged me. "It is because you *are* odd that the girls want you to go. Besides, you will be the first Christian woman they will have actually seen wandering around the hills visiting their houses on a wedding walk. Further, you will be the first *married* woman to attend one."

So it was decided. A walk was what I needed after so much sitting around. These occasions are only for single girls, and it's the one time they can leave their homesteads without the surveillance of an older woman. I suggested that I borrow some clothes and dress as they did, but the answer was a unanimous "No!" They were right: better to remain the foreigner I was and be accepted as such. It would not have been correct for me to have worn a single girl's attire, and to don a married woman's headdress would have caused consternation to an observer from afar, as no married woman would have been walking across the countryside unless escorted by her husband or male in-laws.

They all looked me over critically and the suitcase was tipped out on to the matting; but the assembled women found nothing suitable or pretty enough for a wedding. The only garment that met with their approval among my clothes was a dressing gown with a wide flared skirt: that was what I should wear. Hmid was banished from the courtyard and the ladies ushered me toward Khadduj's room. Willing hands helped me off with the baggy blouse, skirt and trousers and there I stood in nothing more than bra and panties.

"Ooh!" "Eeh!" were the cries of exclamation tinged with surprise as well as shock over my panties (especially), the likes of which they had never seen before. I was turned this way and that for all to get a better view. However, with the knowledge that I would be so indecently dressed beneath my outer clothes Khadduj insisted that I wear a pair of baggy calf-length pants—*sirwal*—and she also lent me a muslin *dfina* which I had to wear *underneath* the dressing gown. Yamna and Khadduj found some necklaces and trinkets, and Arqiya gave me a choker necklace she had made of minuscule colored beads that hung low on my chest like a bib.

Since I was married, the consensus of female opinion was that my face should be made up to Rifian standards; my own was not sufficient. Pulling my lower eyelids down, Khadduj ringed them with kohl. My eyes began streaming immediately, as it had been specially mixed with a pinch of pepper and cloves; this, they maintain, keeps the eyes healthy while the kohl wards off the Evil Eye. Then my cheeks were rouged with a paste made from the lentiscus berry and, for the final touch, I was commanded to color my lips by rubbing moistened walnut bark *(swak)* into them. This produces a rather intense amber shade thought very beautiful, while my own lipstick was disapproved of. My hair was left alone and I was allowed to cover it with one of my more festive scarves. The beauty session was over at last and Arqiya brought out a mirror. I could hardly believe that the haggard, whorish face I stared at was mine. Whatever would Dave say? And thus I remained throughout the festivities and longer, for the kohl and the *swak* were almost indelible.

"You see, you *can* be beautiful," commented Yamna critically, her head poised on one side. Did I detect a barb in that remark? But her expression was devoid of its usual antagonism.

Yamna grabbed my wrist, marched over to the door and flung it open. "Hmid!" she yelled; he bounced out from his grandmother's room and slid to a halt. I could almost smell the soles of his feet scorching. All he could do was goggle at me with his knuckles to his mouth.

"Go with Munat to the guest room," ordered Yamna. Hmid ran ahead with alacrity, not wishing to miss a moment of reaction. Dave had no idea that the women had been transforming my image; he thought I had gone out hours ago.

He looked up from his work absent-mindedly and stared. Then recognition dawned and he burst out laughing, rocking back and forth.

"What *have* you done to yourself? . . . Jeesus! You look like a *passée* madame from Casablanca." I didn't mind looking like a whore, but I did mind looking like an old and ugly one. "This has been done in the interests of fieldwork," I reminded him.

Having got the tip from his wife, Muhand entered the room and we waited for his reaction. He studied me a moment: "Why Munat, you look very pretty. . . Excuse me, Bu Jij, making a personal comment to Munat, but she looks really nice, doesn't she? You should always look like that," he added.

At that moment a loud throbbing penetrated the guest room and I heard the girls calling me; they were ready to go. Dave grabbed his cameras and rushed round to the main entrance to the house while I hurried through to the courtyard.

Although it is quite impossible to take photographs of married women in the Rif, the men had agreed that Dave could photograph the single girls provided they were in a group and as it was a festive occasion. At first the girls were shy, but most of them had seen Dave, slung with cameras, tramping the hills when they were no more than little girls minding the goats, so they soon became engrossed in the rhythm of their songs and forgot their shyness.

Arqiya had draped herself in an extra length of white muslin that partially concealed her face, and she wore impenetrably dark sunglasses, as did her bridesmaids. They were not veiled, as veiling is not customary in rural areas. But as bridesmaids at weddings all used to be veiled until Independence in 1956, the girls felt that the dark glasses were a form of shield and concealment, masking their identity. Thus behind their protection, they became bolder and more daring in their songs and dances, and remained hidden behind these glasses day and night. At tribal weddings single girls are not hidden away; the festivities are a mixed affair, so they display themselves like brilliant butterflies emerging from the chrysalis, happy to be seen at their best by the local swains.

In a colorful stream we poured out of the front door, and as the girls lined up before setting forth Dave had a golden opportunity for picture-taking. Possibly because of my presence, both among the girls and on the sidelines, their menfolk were unusually relaxed. They even encouraged Dave to take photos from different angles and ordered the bridal party to stand at various places within the cactus hedge and in front of the massive door where either the light was better or the backdrop of clouds more dramatic.

The air vibrated to the throb of a dozen tambourines, while the married women hidden in the background trilled and ululated shrilly as the girls broke into song. My heart was fit to burst to hear the chorus that Dave had told me so much about with so much enthusiasm. I was hearing *"Aya-ralla-buya"* in its proper context and its proper surroundings. There was terrific excitement and laughter. The old women, free to mix with the men, cackled raucously as they tweaked at the fold of a dress here and adjusted a belt there. The moment of departure had come and rhythmically we set off, our clothes billowing up around us in the gusty wind.

A final injunction floated over to me: "Keep your eyes open and take note of everything that goes on, especially anything *unusual!*" This was my first experience of the walk ritual and everything was "unusual," so how was I going to know the difference? I laughed to the girl next to me; she gave me a nudge and jerked her head back over her shoulder, winking. "Men!" her gesture conveyed scornfully.

This orgy of visiting is the only time in a girl's life when she has anything remotely resembling the freedom we Westerners take for granted. It is the only time after puberty that she leaves the confines of the house for anything other than fetching water, cutting grass or minding the goats. More important still, the girls were allowed to go on their own; there was no vigilant eye of a father, a brother or an elderly woman. They were *free.*

How the girls laughed and chatted as we walked along and, with the anonymity of numbers, boldly called out remarks to young men working in the fields. They made the most of those carefree hours of liberty, dallying on the way with no intention of getting back until the last possible moment.

It was a beautiful fall day, the sun played in and out of the fluffy clouds, and a fresh wind blew our dresses against our bodies. We swung along the trail to the beat of drums and song, and when the chorus bellowed forth I joined in too. Although I tried hard I could not get the nasal Rifian inflection into my voice, and the girls screamed with laughter at my efforts.

Long before we reached a lonely homestead, the occupants heard us coming and had the kettle singing on the brazier to greet our arrival. The dogs for miles around heard us too, and barked wildly. Every arrival was welcomed with effusive kissing and patting one another, accompanied by a great deal of whispering while Arqiya explained who I was. Everyone knew Dave by sight, if not to speak to, for he had been over these very same hills to interview their fathers or husbands. With each visit our retinue increased. After ritual tea every unmarried girl joined our group and we moved off to another house, in Pied Piper fashion. We walked for miles, but they seemed as nothing to the accompaniment of the cheering music.

The last house we called at was larger and appeared more affluent than the others we had visited. The snarling dogs, infuriated at my foreign odor, made a frightening beeline for me, swirling up the dust as they snapped at my ankles. I swiped at them with the stout stick I had had the foresight to bring for protection—for these are guard dogs and no pets.

We were ushered into a cool room, and I sank gratefully to the mattress, feeling more tired than I realized as well as soggy with tea and biscuits. The ladies of this house were dressed in their best, and the room in which we sat was color-washed in a restful blue. While we waited for tea they examined me quite openly and discussed me as though I were not there, while Arqiya launched forth into her standard résumé. After we had drunk the initial tea of hospitality, a girl about nine years old brought in a plate of savoury-smelling grilled meat on skewers accompanied by loaves of fresh, hot bread. It was delicious, and walking had given us an appetite. This was followed by smaller loaves with aniseed baked into them, which we dipped into saucers of home-produced honey. Rifian honey has a flavor all its own, since its main ingredients are composed of almond blossoms, marjoram and thyme.

Many pairs of eyes watched me curiously as I glanced through my personally-compiled phrasebook. To understand their replies was a struggle indeed, so many women were all talking at once. Blocking my ears to their chatter, I carefully composed a sentence with the aid of the notebook. When I had it ready I said it to my neighbor, who tittered in nervous surprise. She couldn't hear me for the babble around us, so she held up her hand like a traffic cop for silence. There was an instant hush while I forced myself to repeat the laboriously-worked out phrase. No one understood; they were watching me *speak* rather than listening to what I was trying to say. So I had to go over it again and was immensely pleased when, at last, it got through to them.

Gaining confidence and boldness, I dropped an awful faux pas. The conversation had lagged, and other than whispering about me no one could think of anything to say. As it happened, the room we were in buzzed with more flies than usual, and in order to fill the gap and to practice Berber in simple sentences this is what I meant to say: "There are a lot of *flies* in here."

Once the sentence had been understood, the silence deepened. Arqiya looked at me aghast, and my hostess, though still polite, was obviously furious and glanced furtively round the room.

What on earth had I said? I checked in the notebook; no, that's right: *flies*. Again I repeated: "Flies! FLIES!" In fact what I was saying and stressing was: "Shit! SHIT!" Some of the girls snickered but most stared at me with disapproval, and Arqiya with disappointment. I had let her down. Desperately I looked around; there were some dead flies on the windowsill. I jumped up and swept a few into my hand.

"Look, shit, shit!" Earnestly I gazed round at my audience. There was a pause, then Arqiya, who was used to my struggles, gave a squeal of mirth: "No, no! You don't say *"izzan"* but *"EEzan."* She repeated *"Eeezan"* (which is spelled *izan*), drawing it out so that I got the message: the former means "shit" and the latter "flies," and "shit" is just as unmentionable in Rifian society as it is in ours. Fadhma, my hostess, roared with laughter and patted me on the back in forgiveness and the other girls chuckled and twittered around me. The ice was broken and somehow, from that moment on, a door was unlocked and conversation and comprehension progressed rapidly. Needless to say this blunder was repeated and embroidered amid peals of mirth but a barrier was down, and though it was at my expense, at least we could all laugh together.

When we got back I hurried to the guest room to tell Dave all about my day, bursting to get it out. The walk. . . the houses. . . the breaking of the linguistic barrier and the sudden progress. But he barely listened; he was much more interested in telling me about the progress of *his* day. So feeling deeply hurt and angry I went to join the cosy company of the women, whom I had so feared. At least I could have a good giggle with *them.*

5

Striptease and Dancing

As usual, the door clattered open without even a warning knock.

"Today, the celebrations really begin!" declared Muhand cheerfully, although there had been dancing and drumming until quite late in the night and it would go on tirelessly for the next three days from afternoon until dawn.

Men began to file into the guest room; many people I had not seen before greeted Dave effusively. I knew it was time to withdraw to the harem, so I happily collected up the notebook and other paraphernalia I would need.

"I don't expect I'll see much of you, Urse, but *do* keep your eyes open. I want to know about everything that goes on." That went without saying, I thought, and was just about to go when he added: "Be sure you're with *me* tonight. You know I can't work that God-awful flash attachment, so don't get involved in a yakking session." As if I were already fluent enough to be able to *yak!*

Behind the courtyard door I heard the hum of voices, and as I walked in I found it crammed with women in all their party best. Where had they all come from? I had not seen half that many the day before, when we seemed to have visited every house in the region.

"Come and sit over here, Munat; there is a lot of work to do," called Khadduj after I had gone around shaking every hand with many a *"la bas."* "Here, help me with these," she said, pulling up a low stool and pushing over a pile of almonds and a stone to crack them with. Yamna left the group of young matrons she had been laughing and chuckling with and roughly pushed her way into the industrious circle round Khadduj.

The usually placid Khadduj snapped at Yamna as she scattered the almonds. What was the matter with Yamna this morning? I began to split almond shells, not wanting to get involved in an argument, however limited my vocabulary. Yamna spoke to me; I ignored her. "Munat!" She tugged the sleeve of my dressing gown and then rudely flipped the skirt back. What cheek, I thought, glancing round the circle and seeing that everyone was intent on picking up the almonds. Not even my staunch ally, Hmid, was there. Prepared words and sentences deserted me like vanishing smoke.

Yamna tugged at me so hard that the rickety stool I perched on tipped over. It was low, so I didn't mind that; it was her rudeness. Angry myself now, I jumped up. "Don't do that!" I said furiously. She may not have understood the Spanish but she certainly understood the tone. Khadduj's gentle voice was placating as she took my hand and patted the stool. Rwazna, who had the disposition and ability of most plump people to turn away anger, made some joke or remark to her sister which I did not understand. Yamna smiled, put her arm round my shoulder and gave me a hearty kiss. "I'm sorry, Munat. *La bas?* All right?"

"*La bas,* Yamna, yes, all right," and I, too, gave her a hug. The tension relaxed and everyone started chattering again. Word had got around about my underclothes and that was what they wanted to see. Rwazna's cheeks dimpled as she smiled cajolingly. I looked around the courtyard, which was far too public. She correctly interpreted my glance and indecision and indicated her own room, pushing me gently in that direction. So what, I thought, if it pleased them to show off my bra and panties. So with one accord the whole company followed us, even those who had been busy cracking nuts. Like a herd of cows homing in the evening, they jostled and pushed one another toward Rwazna's room.

We were packed in tightly. Khadduj, I noticed, locked the door, though I doubt if it could have been opened anyway with so many bodies jammed against it. Only married women seemed to be in the room, since I didn't see a single *aharraz* (tiara) among the bright, bobbing scarves. It was hot and airless and I was hemmed in and buffeted on all sides by women in voluminous clothes.

Rwazna pushed through the crowd holding a chair above her head. She stood on it and said something and everyone laughed. "You stand on it," she said, pointing to me and then the chair and indicating that I was to take off Khadduj's decorous *sirwal.* I obliged, feeling rather foolish, and grasped my pants firmly to my hips as Yamna held back the skirt of the dressing gown for a better display.

"Look at them!" she screamed to make herself heard above the din. *"Zwinin, dhasibhan"* (pretty, beautiful), and other remarks I didn't understand as some fingered the lace edging and others the flimsy material. I yelped as some plump fingers pinched a hip and heads shook reprovingly. By their standards I was too thin. The young woman who had experimentally pinched me grabbed at her own rolls of flesh through the folds of her dress to show me how well padded she was. "Pretty, pretty; men like fat," and she waved her hands in the air to depict a fat woman. "Too thin, too thin," the voices chorused, and fingers reached to poke tentatively at my stomach. Faces looked at me inquiringly, wondering if I were pregnant. I shook my head. "Not now," patting my stomach. "Three children in Tangier." This statement was greeted with an approving murmur, "Aagh!" I could see a thousand questions welling in their eyes that had to remain unasked at that stage, for I could not have answered them.

As I leaned forward to retrieve Khadduj's *sirwal,* the untied dressing gown slipped from my shoulder and all eyes were instantly riveted to my bra. "Well!" exclaimed those closest to me. Khadduj pulled the strap down with gestures to try it on. "Yes, yes!" clamored others, while damp bodies pushed up to get a better look. Like a stripteaser without music, I removed my brassiere for Khadduj to try. Without any ado she stripped off her dress and had me fit and fasten the garment. She shook herself and swung from side to side, jogging up and down, her eyes wide with surprise at the support such a flimsy item of clothing could provide. Others, too, tried on my sensational garment to feel its benefits; even the ladies of ample proportions tried their best to squeeze themselves into it. The party had virtually disintegrated into a striptease while the room became hotter and the chatter and shrieks of laughter more uproarious.

A pounding on the door and a harsh cackle silenced us. It was Arhimu, and she sounded annoyed and was no doubt wondering what was going on. "We're coming! We're coming!" yelled Yamna, straightening her clothes while I and the other ladies dressed hurriedly. Muhand and Si 'Abd ar-Rahman, who were just outside the door, also looked annoyed and questioned their wives, who just mumbled and giggled.

It was back to work then, and the time just flew, what with preparing kilos and kilos of vegetables and stringing on to skewers squares of meat that had been marinating in oil and herbs. In huge earthenware pots aromatic stews simmered over charcoal fires, while there was a constant flow of food from the courtyard to the guest room. Hmid and other adolescent boys made frequent journies to the river with the mules to fetch water and cut mint that grew close to the river. Muhand was in and out, keeping an eye on everything and making sure his guests had all they wanted.

As is the normal Moroccan and Muslim custom, the guests never finish the communal platter of food, although the host exhorts them to eat; and eat more; and yet more; and so they do, to honor the host and those who have done the cooking. But as everyone knows, there are the women and children and possibly still others to be fed, so no dish is returned empty. On this occasion, extra food had been cooked for the women guests, so several groups huddled over small, round tables to eat in the privacy of Arhimu's room, which was the most spacious one in the house. However, there was a pecking order here, too. Married women had first pick; then the bride and the still unmarried girls; then, last, the children. The bones were thrown to the dogs.

The girls started entertaining themselves, and us, by thrumming desultorily on the tambourines and getting together to make up verses for the traditional songs they would sing during the festivities. It was about ten o'clock that night when the party really got going. The men assembled in the courtyard, sitting in the shadowy light under the eaves. The young bachelors, well to the fore, appeared very handsome in their best clothes with their turbans perched over one eye. With the warning rattle of a single snare they twirled their tambourines high in the air and struck up a challenging beat. The most agile and versatile of the players was Muhand. Anyone could join in the drumming; it was not limited to the single men. Muhand was in his element; in his hands the tambourine became alive, and the courtyard pulsated with its exotic beat.

"Munat!" Muhand called to me across the yard, "come over here, Dave wants you." Then he added loudly in Rifian to shock the ladies, "*Bu Jij* needs help." The women loved it and tittered among themselves, and one young woman, invisible to the rest, called back a bold remark, thereby beginning what was half the fun of the evening. Lewd and earthy repartee, and even personal comments, snapped back and forth. Mishaps that had had no grave consequences were retold and laughed about. Muhand translated the best of them for my benefit.

Dave sat cross-legged on the mat with rolls of film strewn about him, as well as flash bulbs and flash attachment. He swore through clenched teeth as the shutter clicked again and again with no illumination. There was scarcely any light to see by, and although there would be plenty of the same sights ahead of us, nonetheless every lost moment seemed crucial. I peered at the recalcitrant camera not knowing what to suggest. (Even the simplest, most foolproof one still defeats me.) The men, wanting to be helpful, or at least to convey sympathy, breathed over Dave's shoulder, thus further hemming him in and obscuring what little light there was.

Finally, with a joint and careful study of the instruction manual, we discovered that the flash attachment compartment needed a battery. Luckily there was a new one of the right sort at the bottom of the camera bag. We popped it in, made an experimental click, and were rewarded with a flash. However, at that time night photography for us amateurs was fraught with frustration and mostly negative results.

Responding to the rhythm of the tambourines, the girls, three or four at a time, emerged from the shadows. They, too, carried tambourines and, picking up the beat initiated by the men, they began to sing in unison. These songs, all with the same general refrain, incorporated the verses they had made up dealing with the memorable events of the past year, punctuated with rousing choruses of *"Aya-ralla-buya."* To the Western ear, the singing was a nasal whine which tended to become monotonous and, if one did not understand, the verses seemed endless.

The performers, in a horizontal line, walked sedately back and forth rather than danced. Then, suddenly, there was a rapid and lively "dum-dum" on the men's tambourines indicating a change in tempo, and instantly the girls responded by quickening their step and the beat of their own drums.

Two girls, carefully laying aside their own drums, stepped to the fore and, with rapidly twirling scarves, rolled and undulated their hips and shimmied and shook their breasts. The men were in raptures and pounded the rhythm from their tambourines with ever greater verve. The shaking abandon, in which some girls appeared more daring than others, was the Rifian variation of the Arab belly dance.

These festive occasions were just the opportunity for the girls to show themselves off, and it was a chance they were not going to miss. If one of them had her eye on a particular boy who appealed to her, she indicated it by dancing provocatively in front of him, and, if sufficiently bold, incorporating his name in a verse. In this way she hoped that her audacious hints would be taken up by relatives who might then begin preliminary marriage talks.

In the dimly-lit courtyard indistinct figures came and went. It was not considered impolite for those who had had a hard day, or who had come far, to curl up on the matting and sleep with their *jillaba* hoods pulled over their faces. Some retired to the greater quiet of the guest room. When one group of drummers and dancers flagged, others were ready to take their place and keep the songs and beat flowing. The married women watched through the doorways of darkened rooms, keeping the kettles simmering and the tea circulating.

Sometimes during the night, for whatever the reason, the entire scene shifted out of doors. The smoldering coals in the braziers burned with renewed vigor, exploding a thousand orange sparks toward the heavens. The deep crimson glow highlighted the dancers' sequined headdresses; their graceful forms cast oscillating shadows across the ground. At another brazier a group of men squatted round a cauldron encrusted with the soot of generations. Perhaps they were hungry again, or they were late arrivals who had not yet eaten. For there was Chu-Chukth, busy as ever, in the role of chef and still in his workaday clothes.

It was chilly in the pre-dawn and I huddled into a borrowed blanket. Sitting in the darkened doorway with the other women, I felt happy and relaxed as I watched the scene before me. In the jumping shadows the fleshy, oval cactus leaves surrounded by protruding fruit looked comically like feet with toes of all shapes. Some of the tangled cacti were so old that they had almost grown into trees with coarse, seamed trunks; never were they cut down for the seclusion they gave was complete. On the outer fringes of light lurked the usual flea-infested dog, guardian of the house, cowed and cringing, but nonetheless treacherous and alert to snatch the discarded bones before some other half-starved animal grabbed them.

I squinted into the shadows, but Dave was nowhere to be seen among the men who were drumming tirelessly to the singing girls. He had no doubt gone to bed; it was almost dawn. I hugged the blanket closely to me and crept along to Arhimu's room. Stepping over slumbering forms, I found a space to infiltrate myself and was soon asleep alongside my anonymous neighbors. It seemed only a matter of minutes before I was awake again and with eyes half closed I shuffled into the courtyard.

"*La bas,* Munat," greeted Rwazna. In a working dress, her hair still tousled from sleep, she was pounding and slapping energetically at dough for bread. Many of the women in fact were busy shaping flat, unleavened loaves, as dozens would be consumed during the morning alone.

Rwazna inquired slowly if I made bread. I had to answer "No," but to do something I scooped up some drippy dough from the board with the idea of twisting it out into a long loaf. It was too spongy and elastic, though, and just sprang back to its original blob. With an embarrassed smile I gave up; what a useless wife I must have appeared to her—not strong enough to carry water; unable to gut and skin a rabbit, let alone a goat; and worse, an ignoramus about making bread, the staff of life. Rwazna looked at me quizzically, no doubt concerned about Dave's welfare. She wanted to know who cleared the barley of stones and made and baked the bread. My mother-in-law, or a sister-in-law? I explained that it was all done by a *makina* and baked in ovens I didn't even see, and that I bought bread as I needed from a shop.

There was a stunned silence as Rwazna and others who had been listening digested this information. It was a shocking concept. How could I be sure the bread was clean and free of stones? Khadduj's sister Fadhma, who, with her husband, had walked twenty kilometers with a baby strapped to her back, now joined the conversation, declaring that I ate bad bread. That was why I had no meat around my waist and stomach! She clutched the pounds of fat that rested comfortably across her midriff and hips. She patted me understandingly and gently conveyed that they would all teach me to make bread and grow fat, so that my husband would think me beautiful. With much pantomime, she warned me that when I became old *and* thin my man would then find himself a fat young girl for his bed. This was taken as a great joke by the ladies, some of whom studied me critically and obviously thought the time was not far off.

The conversation now turned to Arqiya and the magnificence of her trousseau. With awe they described the two brocaded kaftans and the two silk *dfinas* brought all the way from Rabat for Arqiya's wedding chest, as well as some of her jewelry which had been bought there, too. They contemplated the wealth of a family able to provide a trousseau from Rabat, which, in the 1960s, was at least two days' traveling, and the ladies sighed collectively.

However, despite the material gains, many thought that she would not be happy in her new home: her father-in-law was so strict that not even the children could amuse themselves by learning to play the tambourines, nor the little girls try to dance. Yamna leaned across Khadduj and whispered to me that Si Hammadi was a Darqawi; they were all Darqawis (as was Muhand's mother). She made it sound quite sinister, but it was, after all, only a religious order, although a very puritanical one.

"May the marriage be blessed with sons," murmured Rwazna. She had no children of her own and felt the shame of it keenly; she patted her stomach to be sure I understood. "It's God's will. . . but one day, perhaps. . . Listen!" Everyone jumped up, for in the distance could be heard the rhythmic throbbing of drums and what sounded like bagpipes. We rushed excitedly to the door. The bridesmaids were already outside singing and the women yodeled shrilly, as the wail of pipes accompanying the deep-toned tambourines approached.

Pushing the cluster of women aside, I raced round to the back of the house, where I found Dave setting up the cameras while the rest of the men strode off to meet the new arrivals.

The sound grew in volume, then over the crest of the hill appeared five mounted men presenting a magnificent silhouette. Three were on mules, one rode a spavined nag, and the fifth jogged along on a donkey with his feet trailing close to the ground. Apart from a long, fluted clarinet, called a *ghaita* (and sounding like bagpipes), one man had a strange instrument hung round his neck made from a pair of curving cow horns joined to a single stem with a mouthpiece. This was a *zammar,* which in fact sounded very much like the deep lowing of a cow. The rims of the hollowed-out horns were further decorated with bands of Shell X-100 oil tins.

The musicians were *imdhyazen,* Dave explained as he angled around taking pictures. During threshing time they go about playing at different houses, where they are lodged and fed and given a certain amount of grain and money in payment. They were desperately poor people, even by Rifian standards. People like Muhand, who belonged to a well-respected and powerful family, commissioned them to play at weddings or circumcisions if they wanted to make it an extra special occasion.

The musicians had dismounted by now and were being bossed about rather patronizingly, I thought; in fact the whole welcome was very offhand. Dave further explained that this was because they were entertainers, and largely propertyless. Moreover, for mysterious "racial" reasons such as their "dubious" origins as a social class, they were despised by Rifian tribesmen. The *imdhyazen* were also mule breeders, an occupation which in itself was looked down upon. Also they married only among themselves and were associated with only one tribe, the Axt Tuzin of the Central Rif—whose members, at heart, also despised them.

The players were ushered into the men's corner of the courtyard and seated comfortably on the matting with cushions to rest against. Gone was Muhand's patronizing air, and he was once again the conscientious host attentive to the comfort of his guests. Fragrant tea had already arrived along with a plateful of baked, salted almonds, and I could smell the skewered meat grilling over the brazier.

There was a sudden commotion on the other side of the yard and 'Aisha, one of the bridesmaids, beckoned to me. I hurried over and she grabbed my hand and ran to Arhimu's room, dragging me along. My heart missed a beat, for there on the mattress lay four shrouded figures, deathly still. "What on earth. . . ?" I gazed at them, stunned. A body jerked up and I jumped. A face peeped out from the shroud; it was Arqiya, the bride. 'Aisha doubled up laughing, for she had caught me beautifully. What a fright! I fanned my face with my hand and she burst out laughing again.

"Sssh!" 'Aisha hissed suddenly to the four giggling girls as the women began their piercing ululation, which was answered by others who wound their way down a steep footpath.

"They're coming! They're coming!" screamed Hmid, who had been posted as lookout. He raced into the yard, his awkward, skinny knees knocking together. This was the ceremonial arrival of Arqiya's elder in-laws-to-be, the womenfolk of her future home. Although she had known them since childhood, from this day on her relationship toward them would be one of respect, decorum and obedience. A last girlish ritual had to be performed: "Hunt the Bride," one might call it.

The *imdhyazen* played lustily outside the main entrance while the girls lined up in a guard of honor in front of the bedroom door, beating on their own tambourines. The future in-laws approached, majestically bearing gifts of tea, sugar and flour in stout baskets balanced on their heads. There might also be a length or two of brightly woven cloth and a few trinkets added as a surprise for the bride. As the *imdhyazen* followed the new arrivals, the crescendo of pipes and drums filled the courtyard.

The mother-in-law and the aunts-in-law filed solemnly into the room: they had to guess which of the silent, white-draped bodies was the bride. With crooked, toil-worn fingers the ladies prodded at the bundles amid suppressed squeaks and squeals. The idea was to pick out the bride at first guess, as this symbolized good luck for the young lady. Naturally, they seldom failed, but played up to the game, spinning it out. If they did make a mistake they had to pay a small fine. This was the second evening of the wedding and the last night that the bride would spend in her home as an "irresponsible" girl.

The roving musicians, who had a fund of humorous tales and legends, as well as risqué stories which everyone relished, were strategically placed in the courtyard, where they could be heard equally well by the women and the men. Muhand called me over to sit with him and Dave so that he could translate the jokes for me—when he wasn't laughing too much to do so!

That night the photo flash equipment worked beautifully, but the tape recorder went on the blink. It had given nothing but trouble from the beginning. It was heavy, cumbersome and complicated, not a bit like the lightweight, efficient instruments of today. That night it spewed out yards of tape in which we all got caught, and the light was too bad to delve into the innards to find the source of the trouble. So, for that evening at least, nothing of the music, songs and tales was recorded.

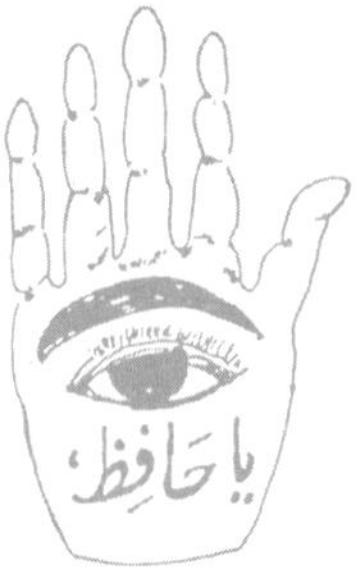

6

Prenuptial Ritual

Could I stay up all night?, Muhand suddenly asked apropos of nothing. Why not! I wanted to participate in everything. Muhand explained that his mother had asked him if I would like to attend the special ceremony, "The Big Henna Ritual." I had not heard about this rite and, although Dave must have known about it, he had omitted to tell me. It is a very private family affair, essentially Rifian, in which even the Rifian female guests were not included; so I felt honored, as a stranger and a foreigner, to be invited. It marked the second night of the three-night ceremony. During the night the older relatives paint the bride's hands and feet with henna and chant a very old and institutionalized refrain as they do so. Even Muhand did not quite know what went on, for the women never speak of it. He just dismissed it as sob stuff for women, as they all seemed to cry. So I was admonished by Dave to keep on the alert: privately, I thought that if everyone cried I would cry too, as I could not just sit by and be the cold observer.

A sibilant hissing was directed at me from the other side of the courtyard: it was Khadduj trying to attract my attention. I pretended I had not noticed or heard. There were times when the efforts to talk were mentally exhausting, particularly when I sensed hostility, which I'm sure I sometimes did, especially from the older women who remembered the days of the Protectorate. And Rifians, both men and women, are naturally suspicious of strangers and above all of Christians. I would often catch the smirks and glances between them from the corner of my eye, and the whispering behind their hands. Then I felt horribly conspicuous (which I was) and defeated (which I was not). At such times I wanted to run away to some private corner to be alone, but the private corner did not exist, and to be left alone in a Muslim society means negligence on the part of the host: both were impossible. Fortunately those moments never lasted for long.

"Psst!" again. I continued to ignore the summons, longing to stay where I was, but Hmid was tugging at my sleeve and pointing. There was nothing for it so, reluctantly, I scrambled to my feet to join the ladies, smothering a sigh. Khadduj greeted me with a beaming smile of welcome.

The room was brilliantly lit by the only kerosene lamp in the house, which threw out as much heat as it did light. Vividly-clad women sat packed together on mattresses and cushions. Yamna made a woman push up on her cushion and patted it for me to squeeze in beside her, and Khadduj passed me a glass of mint tea.

"Bismillah" (in the name of God), I murmured. That, instead of "Thank you," is the polite and normal thing to say when handed tea, or indeed, any food: one thanks God rather than the host in Islamic society generally. My hostess smiled, and there was a hum of conversation among the ladies who had only arrived that afternoon. I caught the word *"Bismillah,"* and Yamna and Rwazna looked at me proudly and nodded as though I were their well brought-up child remembering her manners and doing them credit. From their nudges and winks, I interpreted their words to mean that I would have a far better time with them than I would minding my place among the men. The lady on my right was called Sa'diya, and she started to beat the tambourine vivaciously and to sing in a high treble voice. Another woman holding a scarf close around her hips undulated her body and rotated her belly with no inhibitions at all, encouraging us to join her. Yamna handed me a rabbit-skin drum, shoved my thumb through the hole in the wooden frame, and showed me how to beat a simple rhythm. It was much harder to execute than I had expected; for some moments I got the rhythm and grinned, immensely pleased with myself. Then, maddeningly, I missed a beat and the whole tempo eluded me. Also the small hole was biting into my thumb, so after a while I handed the tambourine back to the expert Yamna and elected to dance.

With Rwazna's scarf tied round my hips and a handkerchief twirling between both hands, I emulated the ladies in their shimmy-shake dance, adding a few extra twiddles and stomach gyrations of my own. Sa'diya jumped up and joined me within the circle of ladies, and to that fast, gyrating beat I improvised some rock-and-roll steps, spinning around so that the skirt of my gown flared up and out.

"Ooh!" shrieked the young women, as though I were their favorite pop star, while others joined in and imitated my weird steps. Their bundled dresses refused to spin about their hips, so my own gown was passed from girl to girl bold enough to have a try. With the screams of laughter and the drums at full pitch we must have been making quite a noise, for suddenly the door opened and Arhimu and her sister walked in, while Muhand peered over their shoulders from the threshold. Arhimu's sharp voice brought us to order and her eyes roved the room, noting the perspiring faces and one young woman still in the act of whirling in my dressing gown. However, *I* was quite decent, for beneath that robe I had worn Khadduj's *sirwal* and *dfina.* Khadduj was as self-possessed as ever, announcing that I was showing them the way women danced in my country and that they were trying to imitate it. She looked past her mother-in-law to Muhand, while Mut bent to straighten the matting and rearrange the cushions. Muhand commented somewhat acidly that I certainly seemed to be having fun and "getting along." After that the door was left open for us to appreciate the musicians and their stories. Yamna pulled a face at Muhand's back; he obviously felt that we were having more fun on our side of the house than the men were on theirs! We then set about preparing tea and late night snacks for the ever thirsty and hungry guests.

No one can sleep when the *imdhyazen* are playing, for their music has such verve and spontaneity and they themselves are such cheerful people. But several hours of the girls' nasal chorus of *"Aya-ralla-buya"* tends to get very monotonous, especially when one does not understand all the verses about the happenings of the past year. So I must have fallen asleep sitting up, and I awoke with a start to an urgent whisper:

"Munat, Munat! It's time." Rwazna's dimpled face was close to mine: the henna ceremony! Everything rushed back into focus, and I jumped up and followed her into her mother's room. It was lit by a single candle and the corners were dark and cavernous, while a charcoal brazier glowed red in the center of the room. As my eyes became accustomed to the flickering light, I discerned Muhand's sisters, the elderly relatives-in-law and Khadduj crouched on a mattress near the wall. Rwazna and I crept across the room and sat on the end of the same mattress.

I was aware of chanting, and the gentle notes flowed over me while I looked at Arqiya. She sat on a chair with her eyes closed, looking very thin and frail in her simple cotton shift. Her bridesmaids, similarly dressed, sat at her feet in a circle. It was they who were singing, and Arqiya's very special friend, Mimuna, was gently stroking her hand.

Arhimu, Mut and two other very old ladies whom I had not seen before squatted round the brazier. Just beyond them, on a small mattress, lay Muhand's old, old grandmother. She was propped up by cushions but appeared to be asleep. The flush of the embers brought into relief those lined and wrinkled faces, protruding chins and sunken lips. Silently, and in turn, counter-clockwise, they stirred the henna mixture in an earthenware bowl. After a time, when the charcoal had died down, Mut balanced the bowl on the brazier and beckoned me over; I was hesitant, not wanting to intrude.

"Go on, it's all right," encouraged Rwazna, giving me a shove. The old ladies stopped stirring as I joined them and I would have preferred to remain a hidden and anonymous participant in a dark corner. However, Arhimu smiled and the two unknown women nodded and patted my hand as I crouched beside them. Arhimu, holding a long-handled wooden ladle, lifted two shelled hard-boiled eggs out of the henna, showed them to me and then plopped them back again. Bubbles broke on the surface of the mixture, releasing an aromatic scent of cloves and cinnamon. The eggs symbolized virility and fertility for the young couple.

Mimuna, the chief bridesmaid, slid over to the brazier and took the bowl of henna, placing it within the circle of the other maids of honor. The old women round the charcoal burner and those seated on the mattress now took up the refrain, while the bridesmaids cried and wailed as did Arqiya, louder than anyone, to indicate her sorrow at leaving home. Whatever one's true feelings, this preliminary and outward show of grief is de rigueur from the departing daughter of the house.

The chant became more intense and sad, like an invisible cloud that enveloped us. Tears streamed down the girls' cheeks as they slowly spread the henna over the bride's hands and feet. Strips of cloth were painstakingly bound horizontally and diagonally across the hands and feet to form a lozenge pattern, so that the henna colored only where it touched the skin. This was left to dry while Arqiya rocked back and forth, as though in a trance, moaning miserably. Meanwhile, Yamna was dabbing Arqiya's head with a perfume-scented oil and combing it through her long hair. Poor Arqiya was no beauty, and now her face was puffed from crying.

It was hypnotic as we swayed from side to side, like seaweed in the gentle wash of waves, in time to the sad, melodious refrain that was chanted over and over again. Women dabbed their eyes and so did I, quite as moved as they. The bride's hands and feet had now been completely bound and her hair coiled around her head. Her maids of honor lifted her from the chair and laid her on a mattress that had been placed near the brazier: her feet would not touch the floor again until she was carried into the bridal chamber of her husband's house.

Sobs choked the song and a fresh flood of tears broke from Arqiya's family as they embraced one another. The prolonged agony was physically exhausting; I felt as if I had cried myself out, but continued to mop my face as fresh tears poured down it. Now the mother-in-law-to-be rose slowly to her feet with her own relations walking directly behind her; we followed suit, forming a procession and circulating slowly round Arqiya's mattress. As we did so, we bent and kissed the bride and wished her health, many children, and a long life in her new home. Then we filed out of the room leaving the bride to spend the last few hours of her old life alone with her closest friends.

Another day was dawning on the new life the bride was about to begin: it was now the third and last day of the wedding. The melancholy henna ritual was over and all was bustle and excitement, though I was still feeling emotionally washed out. I wandered over to the guest room where, strangely enough, Dave was on his own and absorbed in a paperback. He looked up, bright and perky.

"How did it go? I hope you took it all down?" was his greeting as I flopped down next to him, too strung up to talk about it. Naturally I couldn't make any *written* notes; it wouldn't have been right, I remarked, adding that I had got it all in my head. Dave looked as though he were about to say something, probably along the lines of "never trust your memory." But, glancing at me, he changed his mind, and instead broke open a jar of coffee from the provision box and shouted for water to make it *our* way. How delicious that coffee tasted; although it was only "instant," it was strong and reviving. Muhand and company far preferred their own weak brew boiled up with milk and a great deal of sugar. When I rejoined the ladies, it was with a new lease of life.

Arqiya was being prepared for her departure, which was yet another ordeal for the poor girl. Indeed, the bride has little fun at her own wedding! To my surprise she appeared fresh, with no sign of a night of crying, and was joking with her friends. Her warm smile lit up her face as she welcomed me. Would her husband appreciate this quality? I hoped he would, as it quite obliterated her plainness.

The bride's gaily-painted wedding chest stood ready to be taken out and loaded on to the mule. It had been packed with her trousseau and her jewelry, which would remain new and unworn until the marriage had been consummated. What was left of the henna the bridesmaids dabbed on themselves for luck, while the two hennaed eggs, now bright orange, reposed startlingly in a small bowl on top of the chest. The bride would carry these eggs with her when she and the groom were at last alone; each would hold an egg for the other to nibble at, symbolizing virility and fertility.

Arqiya's henna-stained shift was of little importance; it was her going-away headdress that would be a long and complicated matter to arrange. The bindings were taken off her hands and feet and her scented hair was braided into two plaits. It was wretchedly thin and looked worse for the oil that had been poured over it.

"Look, girls!" shouted Rwazna above the buzz of talk as she lifted the hem of Arqiya's *dfina.* "Who has ankles as beautiful as Arqiya, or legs so smooth? Or eyes with such long lashes?" Rwazna looked round the room defying anyone to disagree with her. Her tender heart had picked out Arqiya's good assets; she did have pretty legs and long eyelashes, but unfortunately her warm eyes had filled with tears again.

Arqiya had once more been carried back to the chair, where she sat bolt upright waiting for Muhand to come in carrying the base of her headdress which was a thin vine branch. He bent this into a U-shape, placed it over her head to form an arch, and held it there. The bride's aunt and mother-in-law stood ready to bind the branch firmly to the girl's head and Khadduj waited close by with a length of ruby-red taffeta over her arm. The three women then draped the material over the arch, completely veiling Arqiya's face, and firmly sewed it into place. The rest of the material, of which there must have been at least five yards, was pleated and draped round Arqiya's head, shoulders and one arm. This had to be redone several times to get it just right according to custom.

Muhand proudly informed me that this length of taffeta had been in the family for several generations and had been used countless times as the bridal veil; the quality and color of the silk was richly beautiful. As a final touch, when the material had at last been draped correctly and to everyone's satisfaction, a bridesmaid placed a small mirror in the fold of the cloth on the bride's forehead so that it would glint as it caught the sun's rays.

The day was unusually warm, and Arqiya must have roasted, being enveloped as she was in a sealed tent. With so many women all crushed into one room we were perspiring ourselves as we chewed walnuts (thought to be a feminine aphrodisiac—almonds are for men), drank Coca-Cola, gossiped and shoved children from underfoot. "Can't Arqiya drink something?" I enquired and suggested we could pass it up under her headdress. But I was told by Muhand that she had eaten and drunk before the henna ceremony and now could have nothing more until she was in her husband's house and alone with him; she just had to bear it. Khadduj flapped a piece of cardboard energetically in front of Arqiya's hidden face on the chance that a breath of air might pass through the veil. The rest of the assembled women were quite unconcerned about the stifled bride. They chatted and chortled and made jokes to Arqiya about the marital joys she would soon experience, recounting their personal reactions to their own wedding nights. Nothing was omitted and, through graphic pantomine, the ladies made sure that I understood. Arqiya, understandably, did not find the conversation amusing: she was hot, uncomfortable and nervous.

"Are you ready? It's time to get going!" Muhand bounced into the room followed by Si 'Abd ar-Rahman. The musicians were playing shrilly for all they were worth and the maids of honor caught up their tambourines, beating a cheerful rhythm. Muhand picked up the bride and carried her out to the mule, lifting her onto the wide pack saddle which had been covered with a brightly striped blanket. A second patient mule, equally gaily draped, stood with the wedding chest loaded on its back. Once the bride was settled and her concealing headdress arranged about her, Arhimu came forward and put Arqiya's feet into a pair of embroidered slippers, the only new item the bride may wear.

The wedding party set off. Only the bride was mounted, with Muhand walking beside her to steady her while her male relatives and the bridesmaids followed close behind. The *imdhyzan* played and drummed vigorously until the bride was out of sight, and then, still playing, they rode off over the ochre hills, having been paid off beforehand by Muhand.

It was a long, hot trudge on an early October day up a sandy trail through scented pine trees; the more energetic played "tag" along the way. Dave and I scarcely spoke as we needed all our breath to keep up with these agile mountaineers. I felt ashamed of my flagging steps at the sight of the elderly ladies who strode nimbly behind the mule. Despite the steepness of the path, the bride's escort never paused in their singing nor missed a beat on their tambourines. It was only as we neared the groom's house, about three hours later, that the accompanying music stopped in deference to the bride's father-in-law. As we approached, however, the women, who had heard us from far off, let out a piercing ululation to be answered by the bride's retinue. We streamed into an outer compound, off which the door to the women's quarters opened. Muhand lifted Arqiya down from the mule and carried her across the threshold. As he did so, the bride threw out handfuls of barley signifying that she was bringing prosperity to the house that was now to become her home.

We all stayed outside while Muhand carried Arqiya to her husband, who awaited her in the bridal suite. There, in Muhand's presence, the groom removed the headdress and broke the supporting vine into seven pieces. Once the bride was unveiled and the vine traditionally broken, both men left the room. Immediately the maids of honor filed in to keep the bride company. I was not expected to join them as it is entirely an unmarried girls' party, where they share their secret hopes, fears, confidences and expectations.

Bearing in mind the wedding festivities with their sleepless nights, and in order to allow the bride time to settle down, no Rifian marriage is consummated until the following day. Only after that does the young woman don her trousseau with her sisters-in-law to help her dress. She discards her virginal *aharraz* for a luxuriant silk scarf and silver jewelry and makes her eyes up with kohl. The newly married couple have a few days of honeymoon in the privacy of their room, after which the bride adjusts herself to her new home, her new affined kin and, in particular, her mother-in-law, to whom she must be submissive at all times.

The wedding was over. I went to say goodbye to Arqiya and the bridesmaids, with whom I had had such fun, and we joked about which girl would be next on the marriage list.

We spent another two weeks of everyday life in Muhand's house with the chickens and the clutter back in the yard and myself, at last, mastering and understanding simple conversation. I told Khadduj that we were leaving the day after tomorrow while she was threading beads on a string for Maghniya along with an amulet she had mysteriously acquired. Her daughter had been sick for several days with a fever and raucous cough that sounded very much like whooping cough—a childhood ailment that Dave had missed, and hoped to continue to miss!

"Will you come back?" asked Khadduj, pausing in her work. Then she called out to Yamna and Rwazna that I was leaving on Thursday. They came out of their rooms full of questions: "Why must you go? Aren't you happy here? Don't you like us?" I gave them reassuring answers and promised to be back: it was too complicated to explain about school holidays and having to get back to Rabat. To allay further questions I asked them what they would like me to bring them next time.

"The clothes *you* wear under your dress!" came the immediate reply. "Big for me!" laughed Rawzna, shaking herself and holding her mountainous breasts.

"I'll bring you several, then you won't have to undress to show off to your friends—as I had to! Remember?" Yamna chuckled and added that she had thought I was a very stupid foreign donkey who didn't know how to do things when I first came. We chatted back and forth and I laughed with them, remembering those first difficult weeks in the

Rif and how much I had since learned about housekeeping. Khadduj was rather silent, I noticed.

"Will Muhand be going with you?" she suddenly asked. I replied that he was only going to take us as far as Suq al-Arba', at which she appeared immensely relieved. She did not like it when Muhand used to accompany Dave to El Hoceima for sometimes as long as a week; she was convinced he spent his time with other women, while in fact the worst he ever got up to was drinking beer or wine out of sight of his mother!

Having spent so much time in the busy yard, I felt odd to see it so deserted as Dave and I tramped back and forth packing the Land Rover, with Hmid getting in the way in his eagerness to help. The job done, Muhand was impatient to be off and Dave had already walked down to wait by the river bed. Arhimu, Khadduj, Yamna and Rwazna all came out to see me off and I hugged them again in a last farewell. "And I won't forget the clothes!" I shouted above the roar of the engine. Hmid slammed the door and jumped in over the tail gate, thrilled at the thought of driving to Suq al-Arba', while the ladies stood demurely in front of the courtyard door.

II. Photographs of the wedding of Arqiya, Muhand's niece

The bride (in dark glasses) and bridesmaids

The bridal party outside the courtyard door

Arqiya's bridesmaids

The bride dancing in the courtyard

The bride (second from right) with her closest friends

Arrival of the musicians (*imdhyzan*)

The chief drummer

The bridal mule carpeted up

The final pinnings before going away

7

The Daily Round — A Pressure Cooker is a Fearsome Thing

We returned to urbanization, the family and our friends, many of whom were Dave's academic colleagues who stayed with us on their way to or from their own fieldwork. The conversation was largely anthropological and hence I was largely silent. However, I often heard terms that gave me diverting mental pictures.

For instance, "siblings" brought to mind a lot of fluffy ducklings and goslings, sibbling noisily as they waddled along in single file. In "agnates" I saw a spacious field in the middle of which huddled a large flock of grayish-white sheep. Another term I heard frequently was "endogamous," which at once suggested to me a pack of small and particularly hideous pie-dogs all energetically and frantically fornicating. A further word that I noted was "affine." In this quieter and smoother sounding mental picture I imagined alley cats, with elongated necks, inquiring headlamp-yellow eyes and long pointed ears slinking silently round corners. And, of course, there is "fission," as in "fish-'n'-chips." So really, anthropology was not all that dull! Such were a few of the images that slipped through my mind as I listened in apparently rapt attention, though in reality stringing up these delicious vignettes.

It was February, and over four months had gone by when we retraced the same sand track. The day was cold and bleak when our overloaded Land Rover trundled into Suq al-Arba'. Muhand dashed out of the café where he had been waiting, followed by Si 'Abd ar-Rahman.

"La bas! La bas!" he shouted as he ran across the square with the wind tearing at his *jillaba.* He embraced Dave several times, as did Si 'Abd ar-Rahman, although with more reserve as he was a rather quiet, self-contained man. Embracing and hugging among Rifian men is much the same as hearty backslapping among Westerners who know each other well.

"Munat! How are you? Welcome!" Muhand practically shook my hand off while a couple of vigorous slaps on the back winded me. I gasped that I was fine and asked after the family.

"They're waiting for you—particularly that little idiot with no shame, Hmid." Muhand turned to Dave and ordered him over to the café, as he had some business to complete; then to Si 'Abd ar-Rahman: "You go and load the sacks of barley and the meat into the car and then wait for me." Dave and I smiled at each other; the day no longer seemed cold and Muhand was bossing everyone about the same as usual.

Somehow or other, on top of the barley and everything else, we managed to squeeze in some crates of Coca-Cola and Atlas orange fizz. Muhand lowered his voice conspiratorially: "I have some 'barley water' and we will have a big 'chin-chin' tonight." By "barley water"—Muhand used the Rifian word—he meant Scotch whisky. We wondered about his mother's reaction to this, or even his wife's, as Dave was a little doubtful about Muhand having booze in the house. After the first few drinks he was inclined to become noisy and obstreperous. So far, Muhand's fondness for liquor had been confined to El Hoceima and his mother was unaware of it. We felt it would be an abuse of her hospitality, but just now was not the moment to dampen his exuberant welcome.

As the bottles clanked we lurched up the river bed, much as before, though it was more hazardous from winter rains and soggy mud. Conversation, such as it was, had to be carried on at a shout because Muhand had been given a new transistor radio from a friend working in Holland and it was tuned to Egyptian music at full volume; we could not match such power so lapsed into silence. That year the rains had been particularly prolonged in the Rif, and those like Muhand who lived up river had been cut off for ten days. The debris of floodwater was everywhere and our Land Rover, despite four-wheel drive, got bogged down several times in the mud. Each time it had to be unloaded before we could maneuver it out and so we all became covered in mud too. The worst spot occurred just below Muhand's house, where part of the soggy bank gave way. Muhand's children, who had run down the hill to meet us, were beside themselves with glee at this added excitement. Muhand's youngest son Muhammadi, who was now able to toddle around on his spindly legs, clutched at the hand of Dris ("Amirikani") as he jumped about wildly, splashing mud everywhere.

"STOP that!" yelled his father, in exasperation, but Dris took not the slightest notice and went on skipping around with his mouth half open staring at Dave. Dave looked furiously at Dris, longing to give him a slap. Being curly-headed and blond, he was the darling of his parents and was seldom reprimanded, so now he had become cheeky and spoiled.

"Be quiet! Sit over there on that stone!" Muhand glared at his son; Dris laughed and flung some mud high in the air splattering us all. That did it. Muhand sprang at the child in a fury and boxed his ear. Screaming, Dris at last obeyed, kicking his small brother in revenge as he sat down. Now they were both yelling their heads off and cried even louder when Muhand just laughed at them. Hmid came pounding down the path, grinning hugely—partly in welcome but mostly, I suspected, to see his two brothers in trouble, since it was usually he who received the cuffs. He had shot up immensely since we had been away and his tousled hair stood in wild tufts all over his head.

"How are you, Hmid? Are you still going to be my *'tripiti'*?" I asked. (*"Tripiti"* was his way of pronouncing "interpreter.") He smiled his shy, crooked smile, shot a nervous glance at his father, then nodded vigorously and squelched some mud between his toes.

Some men coming up the river on their way home now lent a hand and got us out of the quagmire while their patient donkeys stood by. Busy as ants, the men heaved and pushed and lifted while Hmid piled rocks beneath the tires. *"Yallah! Yallah!* Go! Go!" they shouted. "Aah!" With a gurgling suction and a victorious whine of the motor the wheels skidded free; I jumped in and we groaned up the same hill that had so alarmed me before.

Arhimu was waiting at the door, and this time she hugged me warmly and even shook Dave's hand—a true sign that we were part of the family, as she had never openly greeted or spoken to him before. I looked boldly at the window and wiggled my fingers, knowing that the younger ladies were there watching our arrival. We felt we had come home. Muhand had been very thoughtful, for in addition to the bright mattresses and cushions he had also provided a table and an upright chair.

"Look, Bu Jij, this is for you so that you can work comfortably." Dave thanked him, as this time he had brought along the typewriter, but he looked dubiously at the chair which was indeed very rickety.

When the tea-making paraphernalia was brought in I got up and told Muhand that I was going to say hello to the ladies, and laughed when I thought of how nervous I had been about meeting them only a few months before. That awful shyness was over and in the interim I had worked hard at Rifian.

Khadduj and Rwazna hurried toward me and we embraced affectionately. *"La bas!* Welcome back! How are you? And your family, all well?" We continued for a few moments inquiring about each other's health and that of the family, known and unknown, as manners required, and fervently thanking God that all was well. Just as I thought, they had watched us arrive and noticed Dave's new beard. "It makes him look old!" Rwazna stood back and surveyed me, her head tilted to one side.

"You've got fatter," she remarked. I probably had, but I knew she meant it as a compliment; being thin is considered ugly and can also indicate that one's husband is miserly over food for the household.

"Tea, Hmid!" Khadduj called out, and Hmid scuttled over with the brazier and kettle. There was a cold wind scurrying round the courtyard, so we settled ourselves comfortably in Khadduj's room close to the brazier. "Won't Yamna be surprised to see you!" chortled Rwazna. She was out fetching water and had never really believed that *I* would return to the Rif, even if Dave did.

"That's right," echoed Khadduj, "Yamna said, 'How could a foreign woman want to live *here*?'" She snorted and we sat silently a moment thinking of Yamna's great desire of all things foreign and of going to France with her husband. Then we heard her approaching. "Hide!" whispered Rwazna, and I jumped up and hid behind some clothes on the door. There was a thud as Yamna heaved the water jar to the ground, then the door was shoved open brusquely while Khadduj and Rwazna appeared to be placidly cleaning lentils.

"So she didn't come back! What did I tell you?" scoffed Yamna. As I leaped from my hiding place she spun round, then ran over and gave me a surprisingly warm hug. Now that we were all together I went out to the Land Rover to fetch the presents I had brought them, including the much-coveted brassieres, a hair brush for Yamna, and various other knicknacks. For Hmid I had brought a red and black spotted football to kick around while he was herding goats; it became his treasured possession, the first gift he had ever received. I gave Arhimu a large shawl made of soft baby wool, and although she said she never felt the cold and thumped her chest stoutly, I later noticed she kept it wrapped around her when sitting in her room.

"Munat! You go away and now you come back and speak our language! How is that?" Yamna was full of surprise and I tried to look properly modest, though pleased that the change was noticeable. "I have a woman from Thimsaman [a coastal tribe of the Rif] who now works in the house, so I learn with her." This information was digested in silence while Khadduj poured more tea. "Did she have a husband?" they wanted to know. "Yes, and children, too." As the husband worked in Rabat all the time, I explained, it was only natural to have his wife and children with him. This was hard to comprehend, as most Rifian men left their wives and families at home when they went to work elsewhere.

"And he lets her out of the house, to go among strange men and enter a strange house? Shame on him!" Khadduj was astonished and shocked.

"Shame on *her,* too!" chimed in Rwazna. I interrupted, and with difficulty tried to explain that she was not a woman without shame, but that when one lives in a city one cannot grow one's own barley or collect olives for oil; everything has to be bought, so *two* people have to make the money. Even the water costs money. That fact was hard to believe. Yamna had remained silent until now. "You see!" she said. "There is a woman whose husband takes her away from the Rif! Munat has said so." Yamna looked at us challengingly.

"Would you let me work in your house, Munat, if Muhand n-'Abdsslam [her husband] went to Rabat?" This was becoming a sticky web.

"You'd be welcome as a guest, to stay as long as you like, but not to work."

"Why not? You help us here." Yamna's quick temper was rising and I was getting too involved in a purely hypothetical question. Even if Muhand n-'Abdsslam did visit us in Rabat (and he very probably would), he would not dream of bringing his wife. I thought for a moment and tried another tack:

"*Of course,* Yamna, you would do the kind of work I do here, we would be helping each other, but not another kind of work; that would not be right." "But. . ." Ignoring the interruption I plunged on: "It would be like. . . like. . ." I sought for an example. "Like 'Aliya!" I waved my hand in the direction of her house. 'Aliya was considered very low-class and she was called in and given all the unpleasant jobs to do at festivities, such as salting goat skins, grinding extra barley for flour and continually fetching water; and she was hardly spoken to.

"I see," drawled Yamna. "The Thimsamaniya is nothing but a servant!" I leaned across and patted her knee. "Exactly! Perhaps, one day, you will come as my guests and friends, all of you, *Insha'llah!*" Then, to give them further food for thought, I added: "You will dress as the women of the cities do, in a *jillaba* and a veil, when we go out of the house or when you drive in the car with me." I continued mischievously and to shock a little: "Not this car that Muhand and Dave drive, but a smaller one that *I* drive!"

"Ooh?" A silence ensued. The ladies no doubt contemplated, each in her own fashion, me driving a car, the wonders of Rabat, the capital, and knowing in their heart of hearts that they would never get there. I wondered how they envisaged a city or what "city" meant to them. In the 1960s television had not come to the Rif, they had never before seen anything more than scattered houses (mud-built) or a market larger than Suq al-Arba'—and that, possibly, only when they were girls under the age of puberty.

"I'm glad that you are here, Munat," Rwazna broke the silence with her own thoughts: "Because now Si 'Abd ar-Rahman won't be in a hurry to go home. He likes your husband, and it has been two years since I've stayed here with my mother." Rwazna gave a sigh that rattled from the depths of her heart. Khadduj looked at her sympathetically and explained Rwazna's anxiety to me:

"She is unhappy because she has no children after three years of marriage. Rwazna feels shame in front of her husband's family and the women taunt her. *They,* and in particular his mother," she continued with scorn mixed with apprehension, "want him to divorce her and get another wife, but Si 'Abd ar-Rahman refuses; he's a kind husband and also he is afraid of Muhand's anger." Khadduj paused in contemplation while Rwazna said not a word. Khadduj resumed, in Rwazna's defense: "I saw her at the wedding. . . *and* heard her. Scream, scream, scream—and whispering. Poor Rwazna!" Khadduj sniffed. "God has blessed me with children, but he has also blessed me with a quiet mother-in-law." Rwazna was crying quietly into the skirt of her *dfina* while Yamna tried to console her.

Thinking back to Arqiya's wedding, I remembered a woman with a particularly strident voice and discontented expression for whom nothing seemed right: indeed, poor Rwazna. I nodded sympathetically, fiddling in various pockets to find a handkerchief to dry her tears. "There, there, Rwazna," I held her hand. "You have a kind husband who thinks you are very beautiful. He won't repudiate you for a second wife; Muhand tells him to be patient. . . So cheer up!" For further consolation to the tearful wife Yamna chipped in: "And what about Munat? She is getting on in years and is still without child with her second husband!" Western methods of birth control were still unknown in the Rif, so Khadduj considered Yamna's remark extremely tactless; but it staunched Rwazna's tears and brought forth a lopsided smile.

The door opened quietly and Arhimu shuffled in. "Any tea left?" She peered shortsightedly round the room as Khadduj got up and led her mother-in-law to a stool. *"Bismillah!"* said Arhimu, beginning to sip the tea noisily. The old lady leaned across the brazier and looked vaguely in my direction; in the last few months her sight had deteriorated rapidly almost to the point of blindness. "Munat, I will soon be able to see again. . . *Insha'llah,"* she added, raising her right hand piously and smiling happily, her face crinkling into a thousand wrinkles. Despite her failing eyes, her teeth were strong and unblemished. Puzzled, I gazed at her in silence. A doctor in El Hoceima, I pondered?

"A special doctor, a very holy man who is almost a saint, is coming to this part of the Rif and I have heard that he has cured many people with bad eyes like mine. Mut and other women have been telling me I should let him cure me. Do you think I should?" she asked anxiously.

Torn between common sense (mine) and strong faith (hers) I did not know what to suggest. In case things went wrong the blame could be laid at my door for having encouraged her. "Well, Arhimu," I prevaricated, "the word of good acts, or bad acts, always runs ahead of a person and you say people speak well of this holy man. Does Muhand advise you to see him?" She replied that it was, in fact, her son who had suggested it and they had discussed it in great detail. Her mind was obviously made up and her voice was determined. Apparently Muhand had already sent word for him to be brought to the house when he arrived in Suq al-Arba'.

"I don't know what he does, except that he blows into the eyes in some strange way," was all the explanation that she could give.

Her daughter was unconvinced: "Mother, I think you should be careful; you are old and a little sight is better than none at all. Supposing something went wrong. . ." "Then it is God's will," interrupted Arhimu. But I was glad Yamna had outspokenly voiced my own concern.

"Anyway, eat your supper now," said Khadduj soothingly, adding philosophically that it might be weeks or months before the holy man got there. "What will be, will be; it is God's will," and so saying she sat down beside me. With a muttered *"Bismillah"* we all proceeded to dip hunks of bread into the vegetable stew—one that, for me, was too laced with pungent homemade olive oil.

We had just finished supper when Si 'Abd ar-Rahman and Muhand n-'Abdsslam came into the courtyard, a sign that it was bedtime or that they at least wanted to be alone with their respective wives; and so saying goodnight I slipped back into the guest room. The reek of whisky fumes hit me like a wall and raucous Egyptian music blared from the newly-acquired radio. Dave was grinning inanely and his eyes were practically closed as he listened to Muhand, who was in a maudlin and rhetorical mood with his arm draped around Dave. He staggered to his feet as I came in and rested a heavy arm across my shoulders, insisting that I share his glass of neat whisky. I was way behind the party but he sloshed the remains of the bottle into our communal glass and flung the bottle forcefully out of the window. Muhand's soliloquies of undying love and friendship were always delivered in Spanish and bits of classical Arabic that he had picked up from the radio, and they became louder and more ardent as the whisky wore on, as did his ideas on sex, his prowess, ability and stamina in love. But there Dave became very "New England" and would not discuss the subject in as great detail as Muhand would have liked. "You wanna go to bed?" he said.

Muhand's eyes swiveled toward the double bed, swiveled back on us in unfocused contemplation, and back to the bed again. Before our joint return, Muhand had decided that the guest room would be our bedroom at night and the bed was actually made up to be slept in. What an honor! The bed reminded Muhand that he, too, had a wife and after giving Dave many interminable hugs and bone-breaking backslaps he weaved his way out through the door and staggered off to his own room.

We felt almost like a bridal couple with the matrimonial couch at our disposal; the brass rails gleamed in the candlelight and the bed was roomy and sumptuous. At the foot there was a window with a solid wooden shutter; Rifian windows have no glass in them and from the outside they resemble the vigilant little eyes with the thick shutters as eyelids that guard the house and protect its inmates' secrets. I opened the shutter to let out the whisky fumes and breathed in the perfume of the night. It was idyllic: no sound of traffic, no gasoline pollution, just the scent of the earth and, in the distance, the bark of a dog, or maybe the call of a jackal.

"Come here and smell this night air, Dave. . . What peace!"

"Huh? I'm almost asleep." Dave pulled the blanket closer. "Just for a minute, it's beautiful," I encouraged. Dave crawled to the end of the bed and poked his head out.

"SNIFF!" Dave sniffed: "All I can smell is donkey shit and there's *always* a goddamn dog barking somewhere! I'm cold."

"Aah, my wonderful, romantic Dave," I commented as I gazed for a little longer at the night and the stars.

Next morning, about six-thirty, late by Rifian standards, there was a knock at the door and Muhand walked straight in. We had tied the satin curtains back to get some air and now struggled to pull them loose about us as he had burst in at a most inappropriate moment. However, he was quite unperturbed and calmly set the kettle and a basin on the floor.

"There's hot water to wash and shave in when you are ready," he announced and walked out again. We bundled into some warm clothes and made our way toward the cactus tunnel for the early morning pee. It was just beginning to get light and the fleshy cactus leaves glistened with a coating of frost. "Hurry, Urs, this is no time for a bare-ass display!" It was bitterly cold.

After breakfast there was the chore of making the bed. It was no easy task, as it fitted flush into its niche and was difficult to pull out. It was a climbing and balancing act on the rails as the sheets, blankets and then the cover had to be spread tautly without a wrinkle and then the flounced satin curtain had to be draped just so: the ladies would inspect my work as soon as the men had left the room. As I had already proved how useless I was in so many other things, I had to show them that at least I knew how to make a bed and leave the room fit for their husbands and unexpected guests to occupy.

The women must have seen Dave trudging down the hill with Muhand and Chu-Chukth, for Yamna and Khadduj came straight in to see if I would go to fetch water with them. Yamna passed her hand critically over the bedspread, tweaked the curtain, then smiled at me; I had obviously done it right.

"If you have anything to wash, bring it along because we are also going to wash at the river." Yamna was picking at the clothes I had left folded in a corner, inspecting them and holding them against herself, but she made no comment as I watched. Loaded with empty water jars, packets of Tide and bundles of washing, we walked down the hill where the river ran in many little channels and selected the clearest one for the drinking water. We scooped out a small hole in the muddy bed and, when the water cleared, let it trickle very slowly into a tin from which we filled the jars. It was a slow process as each jar held about four gallons. No one was in any hurry, since doing the laundry and collecting water is very much a social occasion for women. It is about the only chance they have during the day to meet each other and exchange news and gossip. The children play and occasionally get their hair washed, even sometimes a bath if it is summer. Now the February sunlight was warm and nondescript and birds whirred up from the bushes as we laid the clothes over them to dry. I was surprised to find the water warm in spite of the early frost. Dris was acting impossibly naughty; it seemed to me that each day he got worse. He pulled the clothes off the bushes and ran up the river screaming with laughter as they trailed in the muddy water.

"You shouldn't let him do exactly as he likes, Khadduj," I remonstrated. "He doubles your work!"

"He's my first son and I can't scold him; look how sweet he is!" As Khadduj gazed adoringly at her first-born child there was a ripping sound and Yamna jumped to her feet and in two strides reached Dris and rained some ringing slaps on his fat, naked little bottom.

"Look at what your little horror has done to 'Abdsslam's shirt!" Yamna screamed at Khadduj, and with reason, for there was a long rent in the sleeve. Khadduj rocked her yelling son and comforted him with gentle words as she glared over his curls at Yamna. She, equally furious, was holding up the shirt and displaying the tear to the silent women, who did not want to get drawn into the quarrel. Having met them all at the wedding, I felt that I was seeing old friends again, especially in their daily clothes and routine surroundings. I felt warm and comfortable among them, particularly as I was doing the same chore of washing my man's cumbersome clothes. It was late morning when we collected up the partially dry clothes and helped each other heave up the water jars which were held fast by a rope over each shoulder, and then we slowly trod our way back up the steep path.

The strong odor of cooking oil reached me long before we got to the house. Unrefined, homemade Rifian olive oil has a very pungent and rather nauseating smell; it flows from the jar in a thick, dark green ooze. The stronger the flavor (and smell) the better the oil, it is held. Meal times were an ordeal: with a piece of bread held between thumb and forefinger Dave and I would plummet the bread beneath the oil, as a cormorant into the sea, to scoop up some gravy and a morsel of food, but no matter how careful we were we could not escape a thick coating of that revolting oil. I was beginning to appreciate the wisdom of having a reserve of provisions for an occasional change of diet. We enjoyed the everyday meals for they were spicy; it was just that particular, cloying taste of the oil that became hard to bear. Yet, surprisingly enough, we never had any stomach upsets—thank God! Otherwise the marathon of down-the-cactus-tunnel would have been a nightmare.

It was after lunch on washing day when Dave sent Hmid to fetch me from the women's quarters.

"Think you could do some typing for me this afternoon?" he asked. "I've got a lot of notes to write up and they're getting out of hand."

"You mean type the first draft of that booklet you were planning to write while you were here?"

"Booklet?" Dave looked aghast at my inadvertent flippancy. "I don't write *booklets!* It's either an *article* or a *monograph*. . . God, Urs, you really must learn the garden-variety academic terms if you want to do any work for me: and these particular years I've spent in the field is work toward a major *academic* study. . . *Booklet!*"

"Yes SIR!" Dave eyed me doubtfully: "By the way, *can* you type?"

"Only with two fingers, but I'll do it to help." I was not very enthusiastic; Dave's writing was hard to read and I wasn't used to it. "O.K., you can type a page or two," consented Dave, condescendingly. Impractical as he may be over hammers, nails and anything mechanical or technical, he is extremely methodical and meticulous with his work, so it was with misgivings that I set up the typewriter and studied what I had to do. A head peered cautiously round the corner of the outer door; it was Rwazna beckoning to me. "Come with us, we are going to fetch firewood," she whispered. I pointed to the typewriter, paper and notebook: "I have to do some work for my husband; perhaps later I will come and look for you." Rwazna nodded and disappeared; I really would have preferred to go with them.

Working slowly, so as not to make any mistakes, I tap-tap-tapped at the typewriter, cursing the ruin to my nails on both forefingers. After a while Dave passed on his way to the cave.

"How are you doing, any problems?" he asked as he doubled low to go through the door. I looked over the page in the machine; it seemed all right to me. When Dave came back, he stood behind the chair inspecting my work. I sat waiting for praise. An accusing finger brushed past my cheek and pointed toward the top of the page. "Oujda," began Dave (the Moroccan frontier town with Algeria), "I like it spelled with "WU' (Wujda) as *I've* written it, *not* with an 'OU' the way the French misspell every place name."

"All right," I agreed, altering it to 'Wujda,' then added: "However, except for a handful of colleagues, *nobody* will find these places if you don't spell them the way they are spelled on the map, no matter how right *you* may be! How about putting the correct transliteration in parentheses?" Dave replied he would have to think about that. He read on:

"Goddamn it!" he exploded. I jumped. You spelled 'Waryaghar' wrong! You should know how to spell it by now, you've been here long enough. They're *my* tribe, the Aith W-A-R-Y-A-G-H-A-R." Dave tapped the table sternly as he spelled it out and I sunk lower in my chair, fed up.

"Leaving out the 'G' alters the *whole* pronunciation!" He repeated the name of the tribe slowly.

Light dawned: "I see! You don't say 'Wari-A-HAR' as though you've caught somebody in a misdemeanor; you pronounce it 'Wari-AGH-ar' as though you're gagging on a fly!" I laughed at my own good joke and looked up at Dave in order to share it; he was not even smiling. I doubt if he had even heard me, for his eyes traveled down the page stabbing at every word.

"You can't spell, either." The voice above my head was accusing and my initial good temper was waning too. "It's 'definITE', not 'definATE.' It's a mess, you'll have to do it over again, I'm sorry." (He didn't sound it.) "If there is the *slightest* doubt, no matter how small, *come and ask:* don't push blindly on like an owl in the noonday sun." I was really deflated, having thought I had done such a good job.

Rechecking constantly, I limped along, and froze every time I spotted a mistake—so often the same one. Then, stealthily, so that Dave would not hear the creaking of the roller, I eased the paper from the typewriter, hid it in my pocket, and started all over again. We ended up furious with each other and I noisily ripped out yet another page and, tossing it angrily into a corner, marched out into the dwindling sunshine.

Over the opposite hill some women were creeping Indian file along a narrow path. Though they were all bent over under their heavy loads, I recognized Rwazna by her plumpness and the way she bounced rather than walked. "Yoo hoo!" I waved and went to meet them. I saw that 'Aliya was with the group. She would have been a pretty girl but for her teeth; many were missing and the rest were pitted and blackened. 'Aliya was not yet twenty, yet her face was prematurely old and tramlines of pain puckered her young lips and journeyed out from the corners of her mouth to her cheeks. Life had been hard work from the time she could toddle. In childhood and youth the boys are pampered and have nothing harder to do than herd goats; it is the little girls who have to carry wood, help pound the grain with a heavy mortar, and care for the smaller children, rocking them to sleep strapped to their backs—and most of this before the age of ten. By the time a girl is in her early teens she is already a competent housewife, cook and "mother." After marriage, though, a young woman's health is run down by perpetual childbearing on top of an already hard life. Paradoxically, their aim in marriage—to be a good wife and, later, to wield power in the home behind the scenes—is achieved through having as many children as possible, especially sons.

Such a burden of work in early childhood is the lot of the really underprivileged, but Muhand's family and entourage were upper-class Rifians and therefore their women did not lead quite such hard lives, at least by Rifian standards. "Class" is a mistaken categorization in this case: they were all land owners and as such had an income. 'Aliya and her husband, on the other hand, owned nothing but their shack and were dependent on the landowners for their survival. They were thus viewed as belonging to the "lower class."

At the fork in the path 'Aliya branched off to her home, followed by her brood of children.

"That woman is always so dirty," Khadduj puffed at me as she paused to regain her breath. "Give me your wood." It was a large load but at least I could carry some of it. She looked pale and tired and should not have been carrying wood. Khadduj had told me she was in the early months of yet another pregnancy—her fifth—but she proudly considered childbearing to be her most important role in life.

"I'll cook supper for all of you tonight," I announced on arrival home. "I have a very special saucepan [a pressure cooker] which can cook things in a few minutes." The announcement was accepted in doubtful silence.

"*Can* you cook?" demanded Yamna sarcastically: she still basically did not like me and always grabbed the opportunity to needle me when she could. Rwazna jumped to my defense: "She can probably cook better than you because her husband is fat, not all bones like yours!" Fortunately Yamna, who did not like humping wood, was too tired to bicker about who was the better cook as proved by the shape of our respective husbands. Instead, she called shrilly to her mother that I was to be the cook that evening. Arhimu shuffled into the yard holding a half-plucked hen. Her misty eyes peered at me uncertainly: "How long will it take?" She, too, was doubtful.

"Once it is in the pot, no more than fifteen minutes. . . maybe twenty," I said, for the bird look old and tough. Khadduj smiled placidly as she stared at me while the others just laughed disbelievingly.

The vegetables were soon prepared and set on the charcoal in water and spices which would later be added to the chicken. Khadduj was dismayed that I used only a minimum of oil. "Don't be afraid to help yourself, as we have plenty of it," she encouraged in case I was being frugal. To please her, I added a little more, trying not to get a whiff of it, then went to fetch the pressure cooker. From the corner of my eye I saw Khadduj quickly add another dollop of oil and heard a stifled giggle. Grown-ups and children scattered round the Primus stove that we had brought with us. They watched every move, from spicing and trussing the bird to putting it in the pot and battening down the lid. No one spoke—even Dris was quiet.

"You watch that," I said pointing to the pressure indicator. Gradually the knob rose as the pressure increased. I glanced around and suppressed a laugh. They all had their eyes riveted to the saucepan. The hiss became a high whistle until it was more than anyone could stand and for effect I let it whistle a moment. The women backed away from the stove protectively holding the children, while Muhammadi, the youngest, ran screaming to the far end of the courtyard. Hmid's eyes were round with fright as he chewed a thumb nail, but he stood staunchly beside me until I lowered the flame.

"Now, fifteen minutes," I said, pointing to my watch. Yamna hurried off to return shortly with a large alarm clock so that all could share in watching the time so that there would be no cheating on my part. Though the ladies were illiterate, they could tell the time, no doubt just by the position of the hands.

"Come a little closer, it won't harm you?" I teased, but they preferred to keep their distance, so we sat listening to the clock and the hiss of steam. "It's fifteen minutes!" warned Khadduj. I asked for cold water and Hmid dashed away and brought some back in a bucket. There were awed gasps as clouds of steam rose from the pan as it cooled and the family, on tiptoe or from stools, peered over my shoulder from a safe distance as I removed the lid and placed the chicken in the middle of the simmering vegetables.

"Come, Khadduj, cut it up and see for yourself how tender it is." The meat just fell away from the bones as they tasted little pieces before sending the dish into the men. Arhimu was shaking her head as she reached for another piece of meat: "I can't believe it! This would have taken two hours to cook in a *tajin* [stew] and, now, in fifteen minutes this old bird is soft as butter!" Hens in the Rif are never tender and seldom killed while egg-producing, so no matter how long they have stewed, although tasty, they are usually tough and stringy.

Though the pressure cooker continued to be an object of awe, it was often in demand, especially on market days when the men came back with freshly slaughtered meat which was invariably tough and they were impatient to appease their hunger. Now, with this innovation in the house, a tender meal was waiting almost before they, and often guests, had finished the first round of tea.

8

Ophthalmic Surgery

The frantic barking of dogs woke us one morning, followed by a pounding on the door and a man shouting. We wondered what on earth it could be. An emergency? A death? Dave looked at his watch; it was only twenty to six and still pitch dark. We got dressed quickly and made up the bed, because whoever it was would certainly be brought to the guest room.

We weren't left wondering for long. Muhand was already calling to us. The early visitor was Sidi 'Ali. who was both *sharif* (descendant of the Prophet) and a *fqih* (Qur'anic school teacher), accompanied by an acquaintance of Muhand's. When I heard that this was Sidi 'Ali, who was going to perform the operation on Arhimu's eyes, my heart missed a beat as though *I* were the patient; I was so unprepared for his arrival.

Now that the miracle performer was here, how was Arhimu taking his sudden presence? I hurried to her to find out. I was astonished: Arhimu was as excited as a child would be at the arrival of a very special person, and she had actually put on a clean turban. But Yamna was crying and pleading with her mother to leave her eyes alone.

"I'm old," Arhimu was saying to Yamna to console her, "and very soon I won't be able to see anyway. God guided this man's steps to me, so if he has a lot of *baraka* (divine luck, blessing) then he will make me see. If not, then it is the will of God." Arhimu patted Yamna on the shoulder, wanting no further pleas or protests. "Come, my girl, stop crying and get busy making the bread." The old lady turned to me: "You, Munat, start cracking almonds to roast in the oven with the bread." She set us all tasks and bustled off while Yamna, still sniffling, went out to light the fire under the oven.

After the travelers had eaten and rested, Muhand came into the courtyard to tell his mother how she must prepare herself for the operation. She had to change into clean clothes and then wash her eyes in a mild solution of salt and water. I made this up for her while she was changing, and fetched clean sheets from our room to put on her mattress. Muhand looked solemn. I doubt if he really expected Sidi 'Ali to turn up and, behind the confident front he displayed to his mother, he was worried; in fact we all were.

Arhimu got into bed, very calm and smiling, and squeezed my hand as I tucked the sheet around her. Then I went to tell Muhand that she was ready. Only Muhand and his brother-in-law accompanied Sidi 'Ali into Arhimu's room; the acquaintance who had brought him stayed with Dave in the guest room. As Sidi 'Ali was an old man and very holy, the young women did not have to hide themselves: eight people watched with interest the *sharif's* preparations.

From his deep leather pouch he brought out a thin bamboo stick which had been hollowed out, then a roll of gauze, both of which had been wrapped in a plastic bag. He then produced a small bottle of alcohol (his only concession to Western hygiene), uncorked it and dabbed a little over his fingers and dipped the stick into the bottle.

Pushing back his robes, he knelt down beside Arhimu and looked closely into her eyes. "Look up and out to your left," instructed Sidi 'Ali as he bent over her. With two tapering fingers he held down Arhimu's lower lid and pressed the stick into the corner of her left eye. It must have hurt, yet Arhimu never flinched or made a sound. There was a tense silence in the room as Sidi 'Ali worked; only he spoke, telling Arhimu to look alternately to the left and right. As he blew through the stick, a few seconds in each eye, his cheeks slowly puffed out. He continued this treatment for a while, pausing constantly to inspect the eyes, lifting the top lids and blowing under them too.

"Close your eyes," ordered Sidi 'Ali, and for a few minutes he massaged them with a circular motion. Several times he repeated the blowing and massaging until, at last, he told us that he could feel that the film of skin covering the eyes had loosened. Anxiously we crowded round Arhimu and peered into her eyes.

"Aiee!" wailed Yamna and turned away. Arhimu's eyes in fact looked terrible; they were suffused and bright red, and I feared that more harm than good had been done.

"Does it hurt you?" But she whispered courageously that she only had a headache. The *sharif* appeared unconcerned about his patient's condition while he was vigorously shaking a small flask and, with a medicine dropper, he counted three drops of an oily looking substance into the old lady's eyes. Then he told her to close them again and covered them with pads of gauze which he carefully bandaged into place.

"She must not sit up or move her head for thirty hours," commanded Sidi 'Ali. "After that, take the bandage off, wash her eyes in this liquid here"—he held up a small brown bottle—"and, God willing, the film will have cleared and she will see almost as well as any of you." Then he handed the little flask to Muhand, patted Arhimu's hand and glided from the room with the men in tow.

Later Muhand gave the bottle to me, saying he would like me to look after his mother as I was more used to handling medicines than his wife or sisters. Look after her physical comfort I certainly would, but I declined further responsibility; that her son would have to take on. If the operation was not a success, each one would privately blame me and believe that, in some way, I had "interfered," especially the older, superstitious women among Arhimu's friends.

The *sharif* did not wait to see the result of his work, for he wanted to get back to Suq al-Arba'; from there he had other houses to visit in another part of the mountains. Dave and Muhand drove the old gentleman to the market, while the man who had accompanied him stayed on to gossip and have lunch.

The operation was the sole topic of conversation. I sat with Rwazna and Yamna in Arhimu's room; she seemed to be sleeping, but we talked quietly and stayed close beside her to arrest any unconscious movement.

"Didn't her eyes. . . " burst out Rwazna.

"Ssh," cautioned Yamna, a finger to her lips, for she did not want her mother to know how ugly her eyes had looked.

"Is that how they do it in foreign hospitals? Would a Spanish *tbib* [doctor] have done it like that, or an Amirikani?"

"I don't know, Yamna, but I don't think so. The *tbib* would probably have put your mother to sleep with a special medicine [anesthetic] as the eyes are so sensitive." I thought about the recent operation: "But then the *sharif* did not seem to hurt your mother, did he? And he seemed very sure that she will be all right." The way the *sharif* had worked with complete calm and assurance had indeed impressed me.

Arhimu spent the thirty hours without moving, neither drinking nor eating, though Muhand persuaded her to take an aspirin to ease her headache; she felt hot and feverish and we were all worried.

At last, at the appointed time, Khadduj propped her mother-in-law up against a cushion and removed the bandage and pads from her eyes. I tilted her head back while Muhand washed the lids with the lotion, as they were a bit gummed up and stuck together, as well as puffy. We waited with bated breath as the eyes flickered beneath the lids then opened. Arhimu stared ahead, bemused, then she closed them and opened them again, focusing first on Muhand then slowly round at all of us, while astonishment and joy spread over her face.

"Al-hamdu-li-llah! [Thanks be to God!] I can see, I *really can see!"* and she kept repeating *"al-hamdu-li-llah"* fervently and invoking blessings also upon Sidi 'Ali that his *baraka* remain forever strong.

"Now I will get up." She made the effort to rise.

"No, no, you must stay there for a time," commanded Muhand, pushing Arhimu gently but firmly back against the cushion. "This is a miracle and you must be careful with it at first." We peered into Arhimu's eyes scarcely believing how well she told us she could see. She repeatedly murmured in relief and wonderment *"Al-hamdu-il-llah! Al-hamdu-li-llah!"*

Arhimu's eyes were still a little pink, but not the raw red they had been the day before. Miraculously the film had disappeared. I ran to the guest room to tell Dave the good news and to fetch his shaving mirror. The old lady gazed into it in awe mingled with disbelief, muttering all the while "Thanks be to God! Thanks be to God!" Although she wanted to get up and get back to her chores with her new eyes, she gave in to our insistence that she remain quietly in bed for one more day.

The news spread as if by magic and women of all ages flowed in and out of Arhimu's room wishing her renewed health and a long life, and fervent were the thanks unto God, and the praises for the *baraka* of Sidi 'Ali.

9

Bathing and Birth Control

One morning Muhand announced importantly over coffee that he was going to fix us up with a modern style bathroom—that is to say, a shower. Anything more sophisticated such as a lavatory would not have been possible; the plumbing would have been far too intricate and such material was just not available in the market.

We stared at Muhand, wondering just what he was visualizing. Where would he put it? What about even simple plumbing and piping? And, more important, where would the water come from? The joy of contemplating a shower was killed by visions of women toiling up the hill with loads of water expressly for our comfort.

"I appreciate the thought, Muhand," answered Dave, equally concerned. "It's very kind, but it's not really necessary, you know—and would anyone here know how to. . .?"

"It's quite simple," interrupted Muhand. "I have thought it out: a tin bucket can hang over the trough out there." He pointed to the mule's drinking trough that had been built into the corner of the ante-room. "That will be the bath, and it already has its own outlet drain." Muhand warmed to this splendid idea and was so enthusiastic about it that he insisted that he and Dave go then and there to Suq al-Arba' to buy the bucket and have a tinker make a lid for it and punch holes in the bottom of the bucket. That meant a day shot for Dave as Muhand could not be trusted with the Land Rover alone. He would be bound to take it on to El Hoceima, where he might get drunk and then anything could happen. Ah well, it was all in a day's fieldwork!

Muhand's theory concerning the shower was that the lid would act as a plug. When we required water to run over us we would pull on a rope attached to the lid and lift it slightly, at which point water would shower down through the holes. We were really touched that he had given so much thought to the fact that *we* might find it uncomfortable to wash over a small basin, or with a bucket of water—or rather, a *kettle* of water—a basin, soap and towel to indulge in a grander wash in the cave. The main luxury in taking occasional leave of the field for any small town was to get a hotel room *with* bath (and ideally hot water) and soak in it for hours with a drink to hand.

This unscheduled visit to the market was an outing, so Dris and Hmid came with us and little Muhammadi set up such a brokenhearted howling that he was allowed to come along too. Since it wasn't Wednesday, there was not much going on, but Muhand found the essentials he needed, including a large iron hook and some rope for the pulley. We had a snack of tea, hard boiled eggs and bread in the permanently open resident café before setting back. This was a rare treat for the children, who had never eaten out of the house before.

Muhand had had the foresight to bring along some spare water jars, which we filled from a deep pool fed by a spring a few kilometers from the house (too far for the women ever to walk there). From that day on, it became a weekly habit to take the Land Rover and fetch clear, clean drinking water from the spring. As soon as we returned Muhand set to work: the bucket was suspended by the rope over a beam that jutted out over the trough so that it could be lowered or raised as desired. When it was all installed Muhand half filled the bucket and levered the lid up and down experimentally. Out gushed the water, just as anticipated.

The shower would have been ideal in summer, but then in March the mornings were still cold and the kerosene heater did little to offset the dank chill that exuded from the thick stone walls. I retired modestly to the women's quarters while Muhand appointed himself knight of the bath and worked the pulley on the lid for Dave. Dave admitted afterwards that the whole procedure was a shivering misery, and after a few days Muhand agreed that it would be better to continue in our old semi-washed way until the weather turned warmer.

The ladies, of course, were agog with interest at Muhand's innovation and insisted that next market day, when all the men had left the vicinity, I would show them how we showered, Western style. The concept of a "shower" of any sort was completely unknown to these women of rural Morocco.

"You're going to find it damn cold," remarked Dave—glad, I suspected, that I was going to share the suffering.

Once everyone had left for the market there was almost a holiday feeling in the house, except for myself: I did not want to shower. Plenty of water had been brought up in the Land Rover, so there was no excuse. The ladies sniffed at the soap, shook talc over their hands and examined the shower cap. Rwazna, who was always ready to play the fool, tucked her scarf up under the cap, rubbed white power into her cheeks and swayed around the room in an exaggerated belly dance.

"We will shower too, once we see what you do," encouraged Yamna.

"Dris, stop that!" The child was scattering talc all over the floor. She snatched the tin away.

"We want no children present," I said firmly to Khadduj. "Dris, go along to your granny." He clung to his mother, screaming. I took his arm with determination and marched him to the door, lifted him over the step into the courtyard and then locked it. Dris yelled and kicked.

"Let him scream and kick, it is good for his legs and Munat doesn't want him here right now," commented Yamna, pocketing the key before Khadduj gave into her son's wails.

There was no point in being prudish; nudity, among Moroccan women in particular, meant nothing. So I stripped and stood shivering in the trough under the bucket.

"Hurry, Rwazna, and let me have some water!" The water sluiced over me and I began to soap myself. "More water!" I felt such a fool at having to perform such a prosaic, ordinary thing (in our society) in front of an audience. Though Yamna pulled the lid up and down very efficiently there was silence while three pairs of eyes looked me over.

"Have you really had three children? *Really?*" Khadduj's tone was sceptical. "Of course! Why would I lie? . . . More water!" I was shivering and had had enough of the shower; washing off the soap, I dried and bundled myself into a thick robe. The questions continued:

"If you have had children, then why are your breasts not down here?" Khadduj indicated her waist and thought she had caught me out.

"Because most Western women start to wear those clothes I brought you [bras] when they begin to grow up and especially when they are nursing babies." There was another thoughtful silence as I brushed my hair. I had a pretty good idea as to what was coming next; I just wondered who would ask the burning question and waited with hidden amusement. Married Muslim men and women shave all body hair and especially pubic hair: they consider it most unclean not to do so. To my surprise it was Rwazna who asked the question they had all been so curious and shocked about.

"Why don't you shave there?" pointing to "there." "*Every* married woman shaves. . . It's just terrible, how shameless of you, Munat!"

"And so ugly!" From Yamna.

"How can your husband stand you in his bed?" Three faces stared at me in disgust and bewilderment. "If you have not got a razor, then I'll fetch you mine, then you can be beautiful for your husband tonight." Yamna made for the door and I had visions of myself being held down and forcibly shaved.

"No, please, Yamna!" I had to retrieve the situation, though probably not their estimation of me. I searched desperately for something that would be plausible, something they could understand, however peculiar. "He. . . It is not our custom, he would be angry! He. . . he would beat me!" That was it: "Hold my hair and slap my face!" Yamna stopped in mid-tracks and spun round.

"*What?* He would be angry and *beat* and *slap* you?" the three young women exclaimed almost together in utter disbelief and astonishment, not at the beating and slapping but at our revolting customs.

"Yes!" I wailed, convincingly wringing my hands as I painted this vile picture of Dave.

The conversation faltered on, batting back and forth over our respective husbands' reactions concerning these intimate ways and habits, in particular of Christian people. As we waited for the men's return and prepared the evening meal, the talk was now centered around sex and children and the everlasting question of: "Why aren't you expecting a baby?" And also: "If you had children with your first husband, why can't you have any with this one?" It was a perplexing question and caused much speculation.

"I know why she isn't having a baby," stated Yamna knowingly. "I heard 'Abdsslam talking to Muhand and he said French women do special things not to have babies. He said foreign women only have two or three in all their lives because they don't like children. Is that true, Munat?"

"No! It's not true, we like children too, Yamna, but. . . " I trailed off. How could I explain the economic situation governing large families, the cost of and equal education for girls as well as boys; the cost of clothing; the problem of small houses or apartments; and a host of other things that limit many Western couples. But these tribal women had strong convictions too:

"You should give your husband some children or he will leave you, or take another woman. Be careful, Munat!" Khadduj warned, continuing: "My belly is always full with a baby, one after another! But this time I feel so tired that the moment I was sure I tried drinking *fliyu* tea (pennyroyal mint) very hot and eating grilled pomegranate seeds, but it's had no effect, the baby is still firm. I'm so *tired,*" she repeated and Khadduj heaved a deep sigh as she twisted a strand of hair round her finger.

"Tell us what *you* do, Munat; we have things we do too, but it doesn't always work." Yamna scraped her nails pensively with a knife. She had had a very sad time; her first baby was stillborn and her second had died less than a year ago from what sounded like measles: there was quite an epidemic in her part of the Rif when several children died. In the early 1960s there were no country doctors to travel from village to village or set up shop in the nearest market; it was a question of survival of the fittest and the will of God—especially the latter. For some reason or other Yamna had been unable to conceive again, athough she still hoped for the best and wore a luck charm toward that event.

As far as family planning was concerned: in the early 1960s "the Pill" had scarcely been invented, or was still very experimental, and to explain other methods of feminine contraception was well nigh impossible. I suggested lamely that their husbands should ask mine for a good explanation, thereby passing the buck to Dave.

The talk drifted toward the older children and Khadduj stated firmly that she would never let any of her daughters go to school as some mothers did in the cities, according to Muhand. Then she asked: "Is it true that in France children are sent *away* from their homes to school, and girls too?" Rwazna was incredulous. I agreed that this was often the case in many countries, especially if families lived far from a school. They thought such a practice was barbaric.

"Are your children at school?" queried Khadduj. "Your daughters too?" I confessed that they were and qualified it slightly by adding that school attendance was the law, but that carried little weight; though school is compulsory in Moroccan urban areas, in the country it is very definitely optional and depends entirely on what jobs need to be done, the main ones being herding goats and helping with the harvest.

"I think it is cruel," Khadduj continued. "How can a mother go through all the pain of giving birth to them and nursing them, only to send them away! How can a daughter learn to look after the house, cook, and make bread if she is not at home?" And further: "Who looks after her virginity and honor if not her mother?" Here I was sinking fast into a very complex question! "There are schools for girls only," I said, "and they can also learn the work of the home there. . . and they don't mix with boys."

"That's not enough—a daughter's place is at home with her mother until she his married," Yamna broke in. I nodded. In her own way she was right: it was useless with my limited conversation to explain further against the buzz of disapproving chatter. Seen through their eyes, our attitude to, and acceptance of, boarding schools was reprehensible. The family, as a unit, was the very core of their lives. Children in numbers represent strength, and you should keep them around you.

The women must have got on to their husbands that very evening about contraceptives, for the next day the men tackled Dave for information. "I wish you had told me what you had let me in for; I've no idea what women use sufficiently to discuss it," grumbled Dave. "I could only mumble about it being 'women's business.' They disapproved for the most part, and those a little more in the know had no time at all for the French letter!" he laughed. "You should have heard Muhand! He wasn't going to spoil his fun!" Dave added that Muhand thought women were only fit for housework, a man's pleasure and intercourse: if his wife conceived it was proof of his virility.

Some weeks later when we were at Suq al-Arba' one of the villagers pulled Dave aside and whispered urgently and conspiratorially, hanging on to Dave's shirt as he did so. The man rubbed one foot over the other in embarrassment and glanced nervously from side to side.

"What was all that about?" I asked Dave when he rejoined me in the café. "He comes from the Aith 'Arus clan," he explained. "They are fierce fighters and tough cookies, but they're considered dumb simpletons by their fellow tribesmen. Thanks to you, I seem to have become the contraceptive connoisseur!" It transpired that 'Abdsslam, as he was called, was anxious for Dave to buy him some condoms the next time he was in El Hoceima. He had a large family and his wife was giving him a lot of trouble; she was always tired and sick and was so afraid of having another baby that she interrupted intercourse every time right at the crucial moment. No matter how often he beat her in his frustration, she would not placate him. In his opinion, she was quite unmanageable, nor could he afford another wife; so would Dave please buy him some of "those things" as soon as possible.

Poor 'Abdsslam was renowned for his slow-wittedness and was the constant butt of jokes. However, to please him, Dave made a special trip to town and gave him his much desired parcel the following week. It was difficult to do so discreetly, but what was worse were the detailed instructions that had to be gone over several times.

A period of heavy rain kept us housebound and the river became a thunderous torrent. Dave did not see 'Abdsslam for several weeks. Then, one day, as we were sitting in the sun drying out damp clothing, and when the river had subsided, we saw 'Abdsslam striding up the valley. The set of his shoulders and the way he stamped his feet down on the soggy path spelled temper.

"What's got into him?" speculated Dave, little thinking that he was the object of 'Abdsslam's anger. "*La bas*, how are you?" greeted Dave, but 'Abdsslam was so choked with rage that he could barely answer. He tugged Dave away and I wandered off as though attending to the clothes.

"My wife is pregnant again!" 'Abdsslam's voice and lips trembled.

"That's impossible! You couldn't have followed my instructions: now calm yourself and tell me what happened." Dave led the distraught man to a rock where they both sat down. 'Abdsslam breathed deeply and poked the ground savagely with his stick, an article a Rifian is seldom without. It aids fast and rough walking, beats off dogs and sometimes comes in handy to use on wives or disobedient children. Right then 'Abdsslam looked as though he would like to use his stick on Dave in retaliation for his disillusionment; but as Dave was Muhand's guest that was out of the question.

The poor man's story was hardly believable: after the birth of the last baby, and having waited the stipulated amount of time before asserting his conjugal rights, he explained to his wife that he had a marvelous new Amirikani method to prevent babies. His wife was curious and, for once, willing. "Women!" he exploded. "Do you know she laughed at me when I put in on. . . but a good cuff stopped that. No trouble with her stopping half way through this time." 'Abdsslam paused in thought.

"Well?" encouraged Dave. 'Abdsslam filled his lungs: "After having waited *forty* days it was no fun for me at all! Nothing!" Some response was called for: "How come? Why?"

"Well, while my wife slept I tried to think if I had forgotten anything you told me: after all, who would use a thing like that if it gave no pleasure?"

"So?"

"So I cut the end off—that's what I had forgotten to do the first time. I then woke up my wife and did it again. That's where I had gone wrong, because then it was fine. . . and now look what has happened!" shouted poor, stupid 'Abdsslam, shaking his fist.

Dave bent over as though he were choking on a fly, for I really think that 'Abdsslam would have killed him had he laughed openly. It was a few seconds before he could offer any words of conciliation.

10

A Barren Woman Leads a Woeful Life

Rwazna was very silent and depressed as we did the morning chores of sifting flour and picking over lentils for the stew. Her husband, Si 'Abd ar-Rahman, was getting anxious to return home; he had been away for quite a long time and could not leave his affairs indefinitely in his brother's hands.

"I can't stand it," gritted Rwazna through clenched teeth. "Every month my mother-in-law asks me if I am pregnant. And now, when I get back, it will be quite obvious that I am not—nothing but disapproving stares and no welcome." Rwazna choked on her words and began to cry.

"Patience, Rwazna, God will give you children; you are a good wife." Khadduj was making halfhearted attempts to comb the knots from Maghniya's hair while the child squirmed and squealed. "You'll see." She leaned forward and squeezed Rwazna's hand. But Rwazna was not to be consoled so easily, and Khadduj's visible pregnancy was a poignant reminder of her own failing.

"You have children, how can you understand? Si 'Abd ar-Rahman's sisters sneer at me, and when I fetch water the other women eye me silently or whisper remarks that I can hear about being a worthless one. Oh, how I *hate* it!" She buried her head in the folds of her skirt and broke into wild sobs.

In a society where barrenness is the first and foremost grounds for divorce, Rwazna's in-laws, rightly in their eyes, considered her unworthy as a woman and as a wife. The unhappy girl dreaded that one day her husband's mother would succeed, through constant nagging, in having her daughter-in-law repudiated and sent home. Though I didn't know who she was at the time, I had seen the lady at Arqiya's wedding and she was indeed a very formidable woman with a strident voice.

"She is a devil in skirts!" Muhand often declared, while his brother-in-law sat silent, looking uncomfortable.

Probably the only help Rwazna had been able to resort to had been charm amulets and drinking and eating concoctions generally made by old women well versed in such practices. Urban women often visit a saint's tomb, taking with them a chicken to sacrifice, whereupon he will write them out a prayer invoking God to cure them of their barrenness, and this piece of paper they keep on their person at all times; sometimes, if the saint's *baraka* is strong, they eventually conceive. Rwazna was convinced that a spell had been cast upon her so that she could not have children, and she suspected one girl in particular of seeking the aid of a sorceress to help her to this effect as she desired to become Si 'Abd ar-Rahman's second wife. Si 'Abd ar-Rahman was handsome and well off, by Rifian standards, and could in fact have afforded a second wife without necessarily divorcing the first.

There was another as yet untried solution and tentatively I suggested it: "You know, Rwazna, there is a hospital in El Hoceima for women with your problem, and sick women and babies have a woman *tbib* [doctor] to care for them. Would your husband allow you to go and see her? We could take you there in the Land Rover," and to make it all "correct" in their eyes I added: "Your mother could accompany you, as I will." Hope began to dawn in Rwazna's tear-filled eyes: "Do you really think she could do something for me?" Rwazna's knowledge did not go beyond potions and sorcery, but she clutched at any straw, even, as now, at a Christian one.

"Well, I can't promise," I said, not wanting to raise her hopes too much, "but in my country women who think they are barren go to a *tbib* who knows about such things and often, after a very simple cure ["operation" would have been meaningless], they become pregnant and continue having many children. We can only try."

"Please, Munat, ask your husband to talk to 'Abd ar-Rahman and explain this to him and beg him to take me to the *tbib*. Oh, please!" She began to cry again.

"Come on now, no more crying," said Khadduj sensibly. "You'll go to El Hoceima, you'll see. Si 'Abd ar-Rahman wants a child as much as you do; he does not want to divorce you." Rwazna wiped her eyes and nose, already looking more cheerful. Khadduj stated that she would go too as, privately, she felt worn out with childbearing: "Maybe, without Muhand knowing, the *tbib* could do something for me so that I *don't* have another baby after this one is born." She laughed happily at this possibility. I replied that the doctor could to that too; then everybody would be happy.

We were laughing at the idea of such opposite desires when there was a thumping at the door and a squeaky voice called out, *"As -salam 'alaykum!" "Wa 'alaykum as-slam!"* we answered back. "Come in, come in!" called Khadduj impatiently. She turned down her mouth and rolled up her eyes as she did not like the woman; it was, of course, 'Aliya, who was always cadging.

"What's the matter?" she addressed Rwazna. "Are you crying because you are going back to the Igzinnayen and still not pregnant?" I thought this was rudely impertinent coming from a woman who was not even a friend of theirs, and whom the family considered very inferior.

"That has nothing to do with you, and Rwazna is staying with us until Munat leaves." Khadduj gave 'Aliya a cold stare and added, to squash her further: "What is more, our husbands are allowing us to go to El Hoceima; we're all going together." Khadduj sat down: the fact that she did not immediately put the kettle on for tea was another way of showing 'Aliya that she was not welcome. Athough hospitality required that tea be forthcoming, it would be in Khadduj's own time.

As 'Aliya sat down on the matting beside us, an odor of sweat and unwashed garments rose from her body. She sniffed and wiped her hand across her nose and a sickly baby wailed on her lap; its gummy eyes were ringed with kohl and sticky flies crawled over its face. Rwazna waved them away disgustedly. 'Aliya tried feeding it, but after a few moments of energetic sucking it pushed the empty breast away and resumed a hungry, plaintive cry.

"Give her some tea." Khadduj handed 'Aliya a half-empty glass of tepid tea, and she dribbled some of the liquid down the baby's throat. Tea is the standard replacement for insufficient mother's milk.

"Whew!" gasped Yamna as she banged open the door and swung down her heavy water jar. "What are *you* doing here, 'Aliya? Come to borrow something, I suppose!" This was another reason Muhand's family disliked the woman: she was continually borrowing sugar or oil or a pinch of tea—"to make her own supplies go further," Yamna had once commented inhospitably.

Unabashed, 'Aliya replied: "My husband has gone to the market, so I thought I would slip out for a while. Hee, hee!" she snickered, showing her bad and ragged teeth, absent-mindedly flapping her empty breast over her baby's nose. 'Aliya looked across at me and leaned close. I shifted slightly to get out of range of her appalling breath.

"I hear you haven't any children with this man [my husband]." It was a statement rather than a question for she hurried on without waiting for me to reply: "I don't know what *you* do to prevent that—and I don't want to know!" I stared at her, amazed at her rudeness and hostility. 'Aliya continued, with her attention now on Khadduj: "And if she is telling *you* any secrets, I wouldn't listen to her. Munat may be telling you do so something that is *haram,* forbidden."

Yamna answered quickly in my defense before Khadduj could even open her mouth: "I'm sure Munat would not do that; she knows the difference between *halal* [what is lawfully permitted] and *haram* [what is forbidden]." 'Aliya shrugged her shoulders and wriggled herself around on the ground as though she were a hen settling into the dust. Then she turned back to me:

"However, I'll tell you what a lot of *us* do to prevent babies coming," announced 'Aliya unasked, and she rattled on. But she gabbled so fast that I could scarcely understand what she said, and I shook my head to say so. She continued more slowly but the others frequently had to rephrase what she said: they were used to my limitations and had devised a simplified form of conversation in which we understood one another very well.

"Now *listen!* You're not listening!" 'Aliya was getting impatient; she began her tale on contraception once again:

"If a woman wants to avoid pregnancy, when her period starts, she ties and fixes over her vagina a long cloth which she must not look at for eight days. Understand?" I nodded, and she resumed: "When she washes, she does so with her eyes closed to avoid seeing the cloth, which has to stay in place, also for eight days. When, at last, she can remove it, she still does so with her eyes shut." Yamna yawned in exaggerated boredom. "Munat isn't interested in that, she has her own ways." I wanted to hear more:

"Oh yes I am, go on, 'Aliya." I didn't want her train of thought deflected.

"All right," 'Aliya conceded, shooting out a morsel of dislodged food from the side of her mouth. "Well now, she then puts the rag behind her back, and with her eyes still closed, ties one knot in it for each year that she wishes to remain childless." 'Aliya paused to noisily sip her tea, which had now been made, and to shift the baby into a more comfortable position. Then she continued: "While the knots are tied in the cloth the woman recites a special formula. If she makes a single mistake—a *single* mistake, mind you—the spell loses its purpose and she has to wait until her next period—that is, if she isn't pregnant by then! That's my trouble, I never get through the recitation without mistakes!" Yamna now went on to tell me that when the woman did finally recite the formula correctly, she tied the rag in a piece of skin or leather and hid it where it would not be found. "And of course the eyes must always be closed, remember."

"Isn't it difficult to hide a cloth properly if your eyes are closed?" I asked the assembled group.

"Yes! That is why these spells so often let us down, because sometimes we have peeped without meaning to do so!" added Khadduj.

"There is something else, too," cut in 'Aliya again: "Should any woman find the cloth during that year, the charm won't work. If the rag is not found, the spell lasts for as long as the number of knots there are." I followed with difficulty. "When the woman wants to bear children again, or her husband suspects her of *suhur* [sorcery], she uncovers the rag." "With her eyes closed?" I questioned facetiously.

"Of *course* not!" 'Aliya regarded me scornfully. "I'm just asking in order to get it all right," I placated her. "Please continue."

"Where was I?. . . Ah! This is important: if the cloth has rotted it means that she has become barren; God has punished her for asking too much. However, if all is well, she unties all the knots, recites another formula, and then she burns the cloth."

Gracious! I thought, what a process on top of an already hard life! I had a further question: "Would she tell her husband when she planned to practice this?"

"Are you mad? Do you tell *your* man when you do something like that or about women's affairs? Men *always* want as many children as possible!" 'Aliya's look implied that Dave was either lacking in virility or that he did not assert himself and beat me into submissive child production. With a sniff, I pretended a tear and sighed falsely: "It must be God's will that we have no children."

"Umm." 'Aliya could not dispute God's will, and Rwazna intercepted smoothly: "In Si 'Abd ar-Rahman's community the women talk about a strange fruit, *hantit,* that they buy in the women's markets." (These are markets from which men are rigidly excluded, and they survive today only among Rifians of the Aith Waryaghar.) "It is very expensive, but then only a slither is needed. Do you know it arrests a pregnancy that has already started for as long as the woman likes!" Yamna laughed. "That may be all right for others, Rwazna, but you are still waiting to *get* pregnant!" Rwazna sighed at being reminded.

Later on, when I was talking all this over with Dave—who had heard all about *hantit* from Muhand—he told me that this fruit with such allegedly amazing properties was called colocynth. It resembles a small cantaloupe melon attached to sturdy tendrils creeping across the ground. It grows profusely in the arid, stony belt of the pre-Saharan oasis region of southern Morocco. (I tasted it once and found it extremely bitter-sharp; it left my mouth puckered tight for hours.)

There was a clatter at the door and Arhimu came in loaded with a bundle of sticks. She was so delighted with the recovery of her sight that there was no keeping her at home. She seemed to have regained her youthful energy and enjoyed collecting wood and fodder for the animals and even washing clothes by the river, though she left the backbreaking job of carrying water to the younger women. Arhimu scarcely gave 'Aliya a glance, greeting her only perfunctorily as she passed through to her room. 'Aliya took the hint that she had stayed long enough and got up to go, swinging the baby round on to her back. She hesitated, wondering whether to ask for whatever it was she had come for, glanced toward Arhimu's door and decided against it.

"Heavens, how that woman smells, and her infant too; I'm glad she is not my neighbor!" Yamna fanned her hand in front of her face.

"Do you think 'Aliya practices that spell with the cloth, despite her recitation mistakes?" Her present child was about seven months old.

"I don't know, she is dirty enough to do so," replied Khadduj as she added more charcoal to the brazier. "Imagine eight days without washing!" chimed in Rwazna. I turned to Khadduj:

"Have *you* ever tried *hantit* or any other spell, Khadduj?" Her face closed up and she appeared intent on stirring the lentils. I understood there were limits to the questions I could ask.

"Why don't you go and talk to your husband *now* about going to El Hoceima, then he can talk to Si 'Abd ar-Rahman?" Yamna suggested by way of changing the subject.

Dave was more than willing to put the Land Rover at the disposal of Muhand's family, although persuading Si 'Abd ar-Rahman to allow his wife to visit the hospital was difficult. He finally gave in after assurances that she would not even speak to a *male* doctor concerning her plight, and that her mother and sister and I, if she wished it, would be present in the room all the time. And Muhand added his own extra pressure:

"Are you going to let that harridan of a mother of yours win the battle and shame my sister if she is repudiated? *Are* you?" shouted Muhand. "No, of course not," Si 'Abd ar-Rahman stammered uncertainly, "no, I am *not.*" He stood up with determination, squared his shoulders and marched off to tell his wife of his decision. Muhand was already full of plans: "As soon as it is dawn we will start in order to get to the hospital early, and as summer is almost here we will make an outing of it and spend the rest of the day on the beach." Muhand was in the best of humor. "You know, Munat, that none of my women have ever seen the sea? How can one describe it, the way it moves and bounces and shimmers to those who have never seen anything bigger than the Nkur River? And that, for most of the year, is hardly wider than a trickle."

"Don't even try: that first sight will blow their minds and they'll talk of it forever. . . even incorporate the first awesome view into a verse of a song!" The bay is certainly an unforgettable sight viewed from the plain above: the sea a brilliant postcard blue deepening to emerald green in the shelter of El Hoceima bay itself. Even to us, blasé with seascapes, it never failed to make an impression.

It was a beautiful iridescent dawn when the expedition set forth. Muhand drove with the three young wives in front next to him, the youngest toddlers and a baby on their laps. Dave and I sat with the men in the back and Arhimu squeezed beside the tailboard. ("So that I can be sick," she explained.) Unfortunately, Rwazna, Yamna and Khadduj also got carsick: we had barely started before they had to get down and bring up all their breakfast. And after that it was nothing more than painful retching, which happened so often that Muhand grew very impatient at constantly stopping. He finally rearranged the seating order: we sat in front, a damp baby on my knee, the toddlers on Dave's, and Arhimu sat beside the door with her head out of the window. The other three lolled over the tailgate feeling desperately ill every inch of the way, so they were in no fit state to appreciate the beauty of the first appearance of the sea.

However, despite the stops, we were nice and early for the hospital. We all trooped in, the men leading, followed by their green and bedraggled ladies, their faces shielded by long towels draped over their heads. A nurse led us to the women's section and the men were told to wait in another room while I accompanied the women to the inner sanctum. They were very surprised to find it full of country women like themselves, though I was dismayed at the prospect of the long wait ahead of us. We sat silently for a while on hard benches, and as the travel sickness wore off, my companions began to take an interest in the other ladies around them. Not even Arhimu had ever been to a hospital before. As she was in charge of the younger women and protocol had to be observed, it was she who opened the conversation with another lady nearest her own age. Soon everyone was chatting happily and discussing the variety of reasons that had brought them to the hospital. I slipped out to tell Muhand that we had a long wait so that the men could go and get whatever they needed and window shop. El Hoceima resembled a one-horse Western movie town with no paved streets, and only two shabby hotels and a bar complete with old-fashioned mirrors, but after Suq al-Arba' it was like Paris to us. Also, we had many friends among the urban community who thought us quite mad (especially me) to be living in the mountains, and insisted on entertaining us lavishly in compensation. However, this visit was strictly business: no cigarettes and whisky and the Hotel España; I remained at the hospital.

For Muhand's family the wait was a delightful experience of chatter, shared problems and "women's talk," in which unimagined horizons were opened up. When, at last, Rwazna's turn came up we all trooped in with her to the doctor's consulting room. The doctor was a young, smiling woman who was obviously used to her patients coming with plenty of moral support. When I had explained Rwazna's problem to her she asked us to leave the room; only her mother stayed, as was correct, to chaperone her daughter along with a nurse who spoke Rifian.

We waited about fifteen minutes and I felt very tense, dreading that the verdict would be negative and anticipating Rwazna's despair—especially as it was I who had originally proposed a medical examination. Yamna and Khadduj whispered between themselves, glancing constantly at the closed door. Finally it opened and Rwazna came out; I hardly dared to look at her. With a flurry, the excited girl flung herself at me, smothering me in kisses. *"Al-hamdu-li-llah! Al-hamdu-li-llah!* I'm so happy! I can have children! There is nothing. . ." Rwazna was crying and laughing and almost incoherent, being hugged and kissed by her family, and I laughed tremulously, overwhelmed with relief. Rwazna gave me a card with an appointment for the following week and the nurse, also happy at Rwazna's joy, explained that she would have to spend just two or three days in hospital to have a very minor operation, after which the doctor thought she would have no trouble in conceiving. Khadduj, naturally, had to wait until her baby was born before she could seek help and advice on birth control. She would have a tough time convincing Muhand, who had often said to Dave that he was against family planning and wanted as many children as possible. Yamna was happy but rather silent, no doubt pondering that if Rwazna could be "cured" so, perhaps, could she of her miscarriages. The first step had been taken: the women had breached the hospital and the frontier of Western medicine; it was not the fearsome place they had heard it to be —and at that moment it appeared a happy meeting place where women could chatter together without constraint about the most varied and hitherto unknown subjects.

Hence it was a cheerful, laughing party that set out for the beach and Dave had bought some anti-travelsick tablets so that the rest of the day would not be spoiled. The sea could not have looked more beautiful or blue as we stopped on the heights out of town to gaze at the bay. To the ladies it seemed like a vision of Paradise, at which they could only gape and "ooh" and "aah" in open-mouthed wonder.

We went to a secluded cove and Dave tactfully took himself off round the corner of a small headland so that the women could enjoy themselves unrestrictedly. Though the grown-ups were nervous at the waves rippling in and stared at them in astonishment, the children had no fear and screamed and rollicked and tumbled in the water like puppies tasting the saltiness; soon they were all playing tiptoe tag with the waves and digging in the sand. We happily ate a gritty picnic, built castles and searched for shells which were an unending wonder. It seemed no time before the sun was setting beyond the fringes of the Rif and the slopes of the mountains were in deep shadow, with only their crests illuminated in a carmine glow.

What a day of revelation it had been, a day that had started with sickness, tension and apprehension. No one was sick on the return journey and the talk among the women was desultory, till even that died out as the children slept and their parents dozed. After supper, as I was returning to the guest room, Rwazna walked with me to the door of the courtyard. There she stopped and took my hand in both of hers: "Munat, it was God's will that you should come back to us: first, my mother gets her sight, and I, *Insha'llah,* will soon bear a child. I will never forget this day, *never!*" She gave me a crushing hug and I, feeling embarrassed and overwhelmed at praise not due to me at all, hugged her back, happy to share her joy.

"I, too, will remember this day: it is the beginning of a new life for you and may you have many children and much happiness," and with more strong hugs we wished each other goodnight.

11

The Women Up the Hill

The best time to visit l-'Ass, the site of Muhand's family home, is in the late spring or summer, when the bite of winter has left the air, but it was autumn before were able to go there. Muhand was dilatory in finding out when it would be convenient, always saying, "You can go there whenever you like; I am at your disposition." Finally his uncle had had enough of this procrastination and almost ordered us up there.

"Since neither of your are good mountain walkers, I'll send Hmid to borrow two mules and then we can all ride. I've got so used to the Land Rover now myself that I don't like walking either!" And l-'Ass could only be reached by a foot trail. Not bothering to go to the door, Muhand shouted for his son. "Ah! Hmid!" he yelled, and clicked his tongue impatiently when the boy did not arrive instantly. "Donkey! Come here! He is never here when he is wanted!" In one supple move, Muhand rose from the mattress and stalked out of the door.

There was no real packing to be done except to include warm sweaters with our change of clothes, as the weather could be changeable at l-'Ass, which is higher that r-'Attaf, where we were now. Dave was irritable; he hated packing of any sort and I was determined to travel light and infuriatingly kept taking things out of the bag and generally interfering.

"You don't need *all* these notebooks, surely? And these? Looks like several hundred pens here! Do you *need* so many clothes? They take up so much space!" "Oh shit! Let me do my own packing, will you?" So it all went back in the bag again.

I went off to the courtyard, where I found that Khadduj was also irritable—in fact in a thoroughly bad temper, banging things around. I had never seen her anything but placid and serene, but now her grey eyes smoldered as she shot me a sullen look and pressed her lips tightly together.

"What's the matter, Khadduj?"

"Nothing!" she snapped, and stomped about the yard, picking objects up and flinging them down. Muhand came in. "Get my heavy *jillaba*," he ordered her curtly.

"Huh!" Khadduj snorted and tossed her head, shrugging her shoulders as she turned her back on Muhand.

"Go and fetch it, I said!" Muhand strode angrily over to her as I edged toward the door, unwilling to witness their quarrel. But Rwazna stopped me and squeezed my hand. "Stay," she murmered. "If *you* are here he probably won't hit her—and he often does, you know." Rwazna glanced at her brother, who stood bunched up against Khadduj with his fist clenched, scowling. He looked my way and then let Khadduj go with no more than a forceful shove.

"Do as I say," he growled. But Khadduj was so keyed up that she exploded and flew into a tantrum. With her head raised and her arms rigid by her sides, she gave vent to piercing screams. Whatever was wrong? She tore her jewelry from her head and flung it to the ground, followed by her scarf. Still screaming she tore at her hair, jerking her head from side to side as her thick locks flew about her shoulders, wild as a Spanish gypsy in a flamenco dance. Tears and kohl streamed down her face. Muhand slapped her, not hard, but enough to stop the hysterics.

During this incredible outburst Arhimu and Yamna remained placidly seated in a corner of the yard kneading dough and ignoring Khadduj. Muhand walked out, frowning, imperious and impatient.

Completely baffled, I turned to Rwazna. "What is the reason for that? She is usually so calm." Khadduj, quieter now, was still in a foul temper and in no mood for soothing words. With complete indifference to Khadduj's presence and feelings, Yamna and Rwazna enlightened me.

"This always happens when he goes to l-'Ass." Rwazna nodded in the direction in which Muhand had disappeared. "The first wife lives up there, you understand? You know? Men need it all the time! Every night!" She made gestures. "And Muhand wants it mornings and afternoons, too—*if* he can get it! Understand?"

Rwazna giggled and said that Khadduj had told her that Munad tired her out. To this, Yamna added her own bit of gossip: "Hadduma is really quite old—at least thirty—but Muhand has not been to l-'Ass for quite some time. It's nearly two years since her last baby was born, so you know what *that* means!" Yamna winked lasciviously and made a further explicit gesture. "Oh ho! She is so jealous, is Khadduj!" teased Yamna. Khadduj gave a yell of fury and hurled a pot at Yamna—which missed—and stormed off to her room, bringing down a flurry of whitewash as she slammed the door.

I put in my Western oar: "If I loved my husband I know *I* would be jealous. I'd hate it when he had to go every so often to live with another wife, especially if I were young. Our custom is one wife at a time." Yamna and Rwazna shrugged; they did not have the problem of co-wives. I looked across to Khadduj's door; it was very firmly shut.

"Leave her alone," came Arhimu's quiet voice, "and come sit here beside me. And you two—go to the river and fill the water jars." There was no ignoring the authority in Arhimu's tone. When Rwazna and Yamna had gone, Arhimu talked understandingly to me as I sat on a stool next to her.

"We always have these scenes whenever Muhand goes up to l'Ass. She is best left alone; *I know,*" said Arhimu, not unkindly. "I know, too, what it is like to share a husband when one is young. To attract notice now, that silly girl will scream herself crazy and tear herself to pieces." Arhimu shook her turbanned head in disapproval of such willful behavior. However, feeling calmer now, and with her taunting sisters-in-law out of the way, Khadduj emerged from her room and came and sat with us, though she left her scarf and jewelry where she had thrown them—as a sign, no doubt, that Muhand was not forgiven. Arhimu adopted a no-nonsense voice and addressed herself to Khadduj:

"Now, my daughter, go and tidy yourself up—you know how pretty you are—and then get something ready to eat. The best way to keep a man thinking of you is to feed him well; and you know *they* can't cook for nuts up there!" This was probably an oblique reference to Hadduma.

"You too, Munat: your man needs food as it is a long ride and I must get this bread into the oven." Having given us all jobs to do and bustled round in her customary and commanding way, she had restored the order and tranquility within her domain.

After a silent brunch we mounted the mules from a conveniently high bank and, perched on top of the hard saddlebags, rode off up the same trail we had walked along when following the wedding party. The fresh clean smell of resin filled the air as we labored—or rather the mules labored—along the very steep path which fell away precipitously on one side. Half way up we came to a spring where we stopped and rested the animals and drank from the cold water that gushed from the rocks before resuming our way. It took us about three hours, and by Rifian standards we were very slow travelers.

At last the house loomed into view. "There it is!" called Dave over his shoulder. It was quite different from the squat, single-storied houses I had got used to down in the valley. This was a high, rambling mansion, part of it built in two stories. It resembled an old European grange with its sloping roofs of mellow, mossy tiles, and it was perched high on the mountain, keeping watch over the narrow ravines and the summits of pine trees. This was the house where Hadduma lived with her brood of children, five in all, of whom Hmid was the eldest. Hadduma also looked after Arqiya, Muhand's daughter by his second, divorced wife.

The barking dogs had alerted the men to our imminent arrival and they were advancing down the path to greet us. Bu Tahar n-'Allush Uzarqan, Muhand's paternal uncle and head of the family, led the way followed by three of his sons. We slid down from the mules to shake hands and go through the ritual salutations, then walked behind our beasts up the last rocky approach to the house. We passed through a courtyard (very different from Muhand's) where the golden produce of last year's harvest still hung from the crossbeams, then down a long, dark passage lined with closed doors to a room at the very end. This was the guest room. It was a long, narrow room warmly furnished with a thick wool carpet and divans set at right angles to each other. After the traditional three glasses of mint tea accompanied by baked, salted almonds, Muhand took me to the women's quarters to meet the ladies of the house. There were many more women here since this was the family home to which the married sons brought their wives. What a lot of names to get right and remember! None of them had been at the wedding in Muhand's house, since they beloned to the bridegroom's party, so we were all strangers to one another and the introductions took some time.

Fadhma, the head of the contingent and boss of the compound, was Bu Tahar's wife. She was mother-in-law to almost all of the women, and I was not to see a great deal of her as she was old and kept mostly to her own quarters. Her face was as lined and wrinkled as an old city map and her jewelry of silver coins lit up her forehead like a row of street lamps. The few teeth she had left were as worn as ancient curbstones.

At long last I met Hadduma, number one wife about whom I had been so curious. She was not pretty and was quite a bit older than Muhand, which suprised me. Her large black eyes were sad and anxious, yet when she smiled she showed exquisite teeth, an unexpected grace in such a sombre face. I felt an immediate warmth toward this woman whose life seemed so forlorn and lonely.

Fatima was very young: she could not have been more than fifteen and was married to Bu Tahar's eldest son, Mimun, a man in his twenties. She had dimpled cheeks, a merry expression and was heavily pregnant.

'Aisha was Fatima's sister, a year or two older, and was married to the second son of the house. Her hair was reddish-gold and was arranged coquettishly on either side of her forehead beneath her headdress, falling in heavy coils over her shoulders. A mass of freckles peppered her upturned nose and an impudent smile was accented by large, widely-spaced teeth. 'Aisha had three small children who clung closely to their mother and peeped shyly from behind the folds of her *dfina.*

Among the women of this community were two teen-age daughters. One was a dark, handsome girl with strong aquiline features and a smooth, sallow skin. There was no color in her cheeks at all and her jet black hair was coiffed smooth and gleamed with oil. She appeared remote and withdrawn as we shook hands and kissed each other. Her sister was brunette, too, with wild black eyes shadowed by heavy brows. She had a sullen expression and scarcely ever smiled, or even spoke, for that matter. The nails on her long fingers were deeply hennaed, giving them a clawlike appearance. She reminded me of a predatory bird that should have been racing against the clouds rather that being ensnared in the captivity of the women's quarters of a rural household.

In this cluster of brightly clad women one stood out in particular. She was the dominant character of whom everyone was aware, including myself. Her name was Dhamimund, and she was Chu-Chukth's wife. She was a very beautiful woman whom I judged to be about thirty. Dhamimund had dark, langorous eyes, a straight nose and firm, well-shaped lips. She was tall and slender with a graceful neck that set off to perfection her scintillating jewelry. However did such a glamour girl, I wondered, come to marry Chu-Chukth, a man whom I had seen only in old clothes, doing all the menial work. Admittedly, he was Muhand's half brother, and therefore considered a catch, I suppose, as the family was a powerful and respected one in the region.

I soon discovered his wife to be very intelligent and I saw that she ran mental rings round the other women, as she did round her simple country-cabbage husband. Since Dhamimund had no children and her husband was far too afraid of her to divorce her, she had a great deal of time to embellish herself and dress in her best. The other ladies were content, for the most part, to wear their everyday clothes, generally held together at vital points by safety pins.

Arqiya was Muhand's thirteen-year-old daughter: a gamine of a child, much resembling her father and bubbling over with exuberance and personality and very conscious of her budding good looks.

"I must find a husband for her soon, as she is hot-blooded and becoming unmanageable," commented Muhand in Spanish. "All she wants to do is dance and play the tambourines, and I must say she is very good at it!" Though Arqiya could not understand what her father had said, she knew she was the subject of the conversation and perhaps guessed its gist, as Muhand had used the Rifian work *addjun* for tambourine, for she picked one off the wall, held it lightly above her head and twirled sensually to its rhythm.

Muhand watched her for a few moments, and then reverted to Rifian: "Yes, my girl, it's marriage for you and then you won't have time to twirl to the drums." With that he walked out, leaving me to get acquainted with the ladies. Arqiya, knowing that she had an

ısidered shameful to do so. As she puffed inexpertly,
coughs, she smiled at me conspiratorially. From under the
fished out a very old issue of *Elle* magazine, and we turned
mbed pages together, examining the fashions of several
nair styles, shoes, stockings, underclothes. . . aha! *this* was
eas of decorating came from! On the back cover of the
as a picture advertising a brand of cigarette. The girl
olently on a sofa while her handsome young swain leaned
h a lighter. Dhamimund pointed to the girl—"me"—and
nan—"Chu-Chukth!" We both laughed uproariously, as
in our wildest dreams could imagine her husband in such a
agazine then went back into its hiding place.
ut on the radio and we can listen to it downstairs while we
he said, stuffing out her cigarette. As we went down to
rs, music from Algeria burst forth and immediately Arqiya
et executing an amateurish belly dance.
a whispered in my ear: "It's nice to have you here because
ys the radio for *us*!" Conversation was slow and awkward,
n of this household were not yet used to my inaccurate
structions and I had difficulty in understanding them as they
t and often all together. Hadduma understood me best (as
Hmid) and, to begin with, most of what I said was relayed
We were off on the usual topic.
have any children?" I told them that I had three.
ou got one *here*?" inquired 'Aisha again with a prod at my

ven't been married long," I added quickly to avoid further
uestions.
rried long! But you are quite old! You should have ten by
tions and exclamations burst out on all sides like cannon
d to explain yet again.
arried before, but this is a new marriage."
This information was digested in silence while all eyes
me, my figure, my clothes.
r other husband die or were you divorced?" Mimuna, one
ers, the less sullen one, asked me.

appreciative audience in me, continued to dance, and as she did so, she tilted her head to one side and asked the other girls: "Does my skirt swing nicely? Does my bottom roll?" She pirouetted round, shaking her shoulders. "And do my breasts wobble attractively? Wait till they are really big!" She gave me a sidelong look.

Fadhma, the sullen daughter, merely scowled and pursed her mouth primly, while 'Aisha laughed loud and clear. Hadduma looked up from where she was sitting to comment severely: "When what you call your breasts start to wobble, my daughter, you will be married. And when they grow big it will be with milk to nurse your baby. Now you can keep yourself busy by learning woman's work. . . She's a good girl, really," added Hadduma in an aside to me, smiling a radiant smile.

Of the general household chores Dhamimund contrived to do the minimum, or at least so it appeared to me initially, until I learned that she had her own system. Unlike the other women, she was all for labor-saving dodges or devices. On certain days of the week, she pounded barley for flour and de-stoned a pile of lentils so that she had prepared a supply that would last her for several days. She then had time to devote to her toilette. But she preferred the indolent life and would have liked nothing better that to recline on cushions, haughty, aloof and very aware of her beauty.

Because of this attitude she was disliked by the other ladies of the house, and Dhamimund's favorite occupation was to fetch water from the spring. She was unmindful of the weight of the jar and the long walk, because this was her opportunity to show herself off. Knowing that she was admired, however furtively, she would glance slyly and obliquely at the men working in the fields and this was thought fast and brazen and it shocked the other conventionally-minded women who accompanied her. In their heart of hearts they too, no doubt, would have liked to flaunt themselves!

Unlike at Muhand's house, here the wives had a big, communal living room which was dominated by an immense fireplace where, in a heap of hot ashes, smoldered a fire that had probably been lit generations ago and had never truly gone out. Various blackened pots were simmering around it and the whole room was cosy, warm and lived-in. The women also had their own separate quarters, but it was in this room that they appeared to spend most of the day.

"Come and sit down," invited Hadduma, placing a bolster near the fire for me. The children, overexcited, pushed and bumped into each other, touching me and then running away. "Out of the way with you! Go on!" Hadduma shooed them away unconvincingly, buy they were soon back. "You must excuse them, they have no manners; they are no better than donkeys," she added politely, not wishing me to feel that I was a curiosity because I was the first foreign woman to visit the house . . . and in such strange clothes!

This remark, though directed at the children, was a hint to the others to stop staring at me and whispering, for they suddenly remembered their own manners and bustled about assembling the accoutrements for tea and putting out nuts and biscuits to eat with it. That first day I was allowed to be a guest. There was a brief pause while Hadduma blew up the fire with a pair of ornate bellows during which I felt myself being covertly studied.

"Tell me your name again," I said to the girl next to me to start some conversation.

"Fatima," she replied, scarcely above a whisper. Pointing to each person in turn I went slowly round the circle getting the names once more firmly fixed in my mind. With each woman I had made a mental note of some physical attribute, or detail of clothing, so that I would remember the right name with the right face.

"What is *your* name?" inquired Dhamimund.

"Munat," I answered.

"No, your real name, your foreign name," she insisted.

"Ursula. Ur-su-la," I repeated slowly. They all tried saying it, even some of the children, giggling after their efforts, but I was glad that they stuck to "Munat." I had become used to it and liked the name, anyway, and it was a familiar one to them.

Fatima, the very young wife, handed me some biscuits then helped herself to three, laughing. "I get so hungry these days," and she patted her stomach. "When do you expect your baby?" I asked. The young woman was very large and I reckoned her time could not be far off.

"In about five months," was her astonishing reply. "It has started to kick and is so strong that is will be a boy, I am sure, *Insha'llah!"*

"Perhaps it will be boy twins," I suggested to please her, as the birth of twins of either sex is considered unusually lucky.

As I looked around the room I
wooden gallery, part of which wa
with a brown motif worked into i
"That is where I live. Would
invitingly.
In the ensuing silence I sens
understand, but knew, too, that I w
"Excuse me for just a short
general, and Dhamimund, with he
rickety stairs. She drew aside the
and stepped onto the bright carpet
Instead of the garish floral-
covered with lengths of wooll
cushions. At hand, were two low
smoked like a chimney), and a bra
I could see that Dhamimund w
constant polishing. It was a mo
who had never been out of the Ri
almost as though Dhamimund ha
on Interior Design for the Rural
surprised to have seen one lying
Dhamimund could not read and
urban or Western women.
From a miscellany of orn
powered by old-fashioned glass v
early 1960's were still a novelty
the average pocket because of th
been given to Chu-Chukth by a
newspaper and newscarrier for th
point of the room, for it rested on
"How pretty!" was all I said
is not correct to admire an obje
since they, in duty-bound hosp
After a while I rummaged in my
felt I could smoke without sh
jokingly and to my astonishm
make sure the curtain was tightl

and it is c
smothering
mattress sh
the well-th
years ago—
where the
magazine
reclined in
over her w
then to the
neither of u
role. The n
"I will
drink tea,"
join the oth
was on her
Haddu
she never p
as the wom
sentence co
spoke so fa
did her son,
through her
"Do yo
"Have
stomach.
"No, I
complicated
"Not m
now!" Que
shots, so I h
"I was
"Aah!"
contemplate
"Did yo
of the daugh

"I was divorced," I replied abruptly; this conversation was beginning to irritate.

"But why were you divorced if you gave him children? Or did he want more sons? In time, you might have had more. . . " Hadduma studied me anxiously; although she was not divorced, her marriage to Muhand amounted almost to a separation.

"There must have been a reason!" insisted Mimuna, who was unduly curious about my marital affairs on such short acquaintance. Her sister Fadhma never said a word, but just stared at me.

What could I reply concerning all the complex reasons for divorce in a Western society? What , if any, part of it would be remotely comprehensible to these women whose world was so small and enclosed? All that I could think of to say was that my former husband had found me extremely bad tempered.

"Hee, hee, hee!" tittered 'Aisha. "At least you are honest about yourself!"

"And clever, too, if this man hasn't found out!" added Dhamimund slyly.

Fortunately further conversaion of husbands, babies and sex was interrupted by Muhand opening the door and saying that Dave wanted me in the guest room. The group came with me to the door, the children pushing past me into the passage.

"Come back again soon!"

"You are always welcome here, any time!"

"Just walk in when you please!"

"Thank you, thank you!" I replied as I shook hands with each one, even though I was only going just down the passage. In the guest room I found Dave packing away his notes.

"How was it? Do you find you're more at ease now? Though you must try to be impartial; you've got a bigger crowd of women and their personalities to deal with." He was right. In that short time I had already felt the tremendous undercurrent of tension and jealousy, especially toward Dhamimund, who, apart from being bright, was very unconventional. I told Dave about the copy of *Elle* under the mattress, the cigarette ad and the fact that she even had a smoke with me!

"Most of the men think she is fast and rather bad news, though I think that secretly they envy Chu-Chukth. She's very beautiful, I hear." Dave added that Dhamimund came from a community famous for the beauty of its women. The fact that she didn't "belong" accounted for much of her unpopularity. But how Chu-Chukth had managed to get himself such an intelligent beauty I never found out. A good alliance of families, obviously.

In this big, rambling house, Dave and I actually had a room to ourselves; several folded carpets formed our mattress and with our sleeping bags added we had a very comfortable bed. As in all country communities we turned in early, but fortunately for us there was a lamp to spare so that we could read until we were sleepy. It seemed the middle of the night when I was woken by a regular, even thud, thud, thud.

"What's that?" I nudged Dave awake. "What?" he mumbled, sleepily burrowing into the blankets.

"What's that thudding and vibrating?" Dave listened.

"Oh shit! We must be right over the women's room; that noise is going to wake us every morning. It's somebody pounding grain. But you don't have to get up." Nor did I feel like it that morning. That sound woke us every morning long before it was light, so one day, being more accustomed to the house and its inmates, I got up and dressed and felt my way down the long passage to see who was at work so early. Also I felt a little guilty at being the only woman who stayed in bed till after the sun was up. I tapped on the big, heavy door that shut off this room from the rest of the house.

"Come in!" called a muffled voice without a pause in the thudding. There Hadduma sat in front of the fire without her headscarf, her hair still in disheveled braids. It was only just after five and she was already at work making flour for the early bread. No one was up yet and there was nothing for me to do so I sat down.

"Good morning! *La bas?* All well?"

"And good morning to you! *La bas?* All is well, *Al- hamdu-li-llah!*"

"Can I help with anything? Clean lentils?" Hadduma chuckled indulgently as to a child and smiled at me with a warmth and friendliness that quite lit up her face, though the sadness never completely left her eyes. She handed me a sieve to sift the flour, which she tipped from the heavy wooden mortar. The mortar was a stout hollowed-out olive branch about three feet high that had become smooth and shiny with generations of use. The pestle had also been carved from a branch and was equally smooth and polished. An earthenware bowl rested in the ashes, so I lifted the lid curiously and saw that it contained porridge simmering for breakfast. The ladle was also made from olive wood and had a pattern worked carefully along the handle. It was things like that that were so pleasing about this house; most of the utensils were made of wood or pottery, there was very little plastic in use, everyone lived comfortably and in style, as they had for generations.

I commented about the carving and graceful shape of the spoon. "Did you make this?" Hadduma nodded. Her twenty-month old baby crawled into my lap, chewing on a cinder to sooth its gums.

"Don't you have things like that in your house?"

"No, not with drawings on them. Our things are made by machine; our spoons are mostly metal." Hadduma nodded understandingly. "Muhand likes metal, too, and plastic for bowls." It was true that I had seen a lot of plastic in the other house, without giving it much thought. Muhand scorned the old-fashioned things. The only popular plastic article in this house were plastic sandals, which all the women wore.

Later other sleepy, tousled wives came to pound their own barley. They pushed the toddlers out of doors to relieve themselves and then fed them round the warmth of the fire.

"Good morning, Munat! *La bas?* All well?" they called out cheerfully and we went through the rigamarole of salutations.

"Why are you up so early?" asked 'Aisha, not really wanting an answer. Her hair flowed about her shoulders in a copper stream. Clutching at a thick strand she pulled a heavy comb through it; how beautiful her husband must find her, I thought.

"Agh! My hair is so thick I get an arm ache combing through it!" And she threw the comb into the corner of the room. "I'll do your hair for you," I said, and hurried off to fetch my strong hairbrush. A laughing hour was spent in brushing the tangles for everyone and even the children with a few squeals joined in the act.

The ladies of the house were getting used to me and I to them. Though they poked and pinched me it was more for curiosity and the laughter was good-natured. I was rather like a strange pet, shown-off or tolerated. That awful shyness-cum-fear had gone; being able to communicate, however badly, made all the difference. Now I was able to laugh with them as they fingered the material of my clothes, peeped beneath my skirt and were hugely intrigued by my stockings—and thick wool at that. And I, too, could tease them and finger back *their* clothes.

After the first visit I had adapted my wardrobe to suit their tastes and went around in full, long skirts or a long dress, clothing that was not particularly practical in rough country but jeans or trousers alone would have been a scandal. For any festive occasion that might come up, I had strings of beads and a fancy skirt and blouse as well as a *dfina* of my own that I had brought along. The little gold or silver jewelry I had I left at home, not through fear of it being stolen in the Rif—that would never happen—but because I might lose it. One thing none of the women could ever understand was why I had no gold or silver to display with my daily attire, as they did. In their view Dave was a rich man; he owned a large car (the Land Rover, which was technically the property of the American Museum of Natural History, from which Dave had received a grant), several cameras, a music/talking machine (tape recorder), as well as several changes of shirts, socks and two pairs of trousers. The laundry was visible on wash days and details of the other possessions they obtained from their husbands. I think that they thought him just plain mean and pitied my lot. Many was the sympathetic pat I received as a woman silently examined the single silver bracelet that never left my arm, or fingered the cheap beads around my neck. They shook their heads in commiseration; my lot, perhaps, was not such a happy one: a stingy husband and the ill luck to have no children by him!

III. Photographs taken at the Upper House in the mountain community of l-‘Ass

Bu Tahar Uzarqan, head of the family and household

Fadhma, Bu Tahar's wife and head of the women's compound

Corner of the family house at l-‘Ass

Hadduma, Muhand's first wife, with two daughters

One of the unmarried sisters

Mimuna's shy daughters

'Aisha's small daughter

Arqiya, Muhand's frivolous daughter

Maghniya before the scorpion sting

Olive wood, mortar and pestle

Dhamimund and her water jugs

The valley of the spring

Plowing a steep hill

Hmid herding goats

The bridegroom

Muhand learning to use a camera

Tea drinking during a plowing break

12

A Woman's Place Is In the Home

Dave and I did a lot of walking round l-'Ass, for the coolness was invigorating and the air tangy with the scent of Aleppo pine. Fields of barley potatoes and corn clung to hills so steep that I wondered how they had ever been ploughed.

The first house that we visited a few days after our arrival in l-'Ass was that of Hammadi, who lived about three miles away. This was the house that Arqiya had been taken to as a bride and its owner would have been most upset had we visited anyone else first. We went to several other houses too, but most of the men were out busy in the fields and, with only the women at home, Dave did not want the men dragged from work to entertain in their guest room. As a rule they came to Bu Tahar's house in the evenings to visit with him and discuss the latest happenings in the community.

Muhand was not very happy among his senior kinsmen, since it was not his place to speak and command, but rather to listen and obey. Such a situation chafed his independent spirit and he bore these visits to l-'Ass with ill grace. He was offhand and insolent, if not actually rude, and kept slipping in snide remarks to Dave in Spanish of a derogatory nature, which embarrassed us. Reluctantly Muhand accompanied us to the house of Hammadi, who received us with his habitual gracious reserve.

"*'Abdsslam!*" he called as he led the way to the guest room and a boy came through the door that shut off the women's quarters. Hammadi said something which I did not catch and the child hurried away. Barely had we sat down when Arhma, Hammadi's wife, rushed in. She greeted Dave, then me. Being old, she was free to come and go as she liked and even to sit with us in the guest room if she cared to, though very few ever did that.

"Come on, Munat, Arqiya is dying to see you, for we heard you had come to l-'Ass." Arhimu grabbed my hand and we went off to say hello to the ladies. Arqiya and I hugged each other like old friends, as indeed I felt we were. As I looked at her I could hardly believe my eyes: the plain, thin little bridal mouse had now blossomed forth into a beautiful flower; marriage had filled out and matured her body and the slight plumpness suited her. She seemed very happy. Her bright headscarf and silver medallions lent color and warmth to her skin and her eyes looked greener that ever.

"I never knew you had such beautiful eyes, Arqiya; makeup really suits you!" She had colored her lips with walnut bark, which highlighted the very attractive mouth; in fact she had become quite a beauty. She got along well with her mother-in-law, who, despite her strong character, was a very kind woman.

I was introduced to the other young women with whom Arqiya now shared her home: Maghniya, Hadda and Mimuna. Maghniya had four children and was married to Hammadi's eldest son. Hadda was also married to another of Hammadi's sons, while Mimuna was a cousin of Arqiya, and I never did figure out who her husband was.

"Don't stare!" admonished Arqiya. "Haven't you seen a foreign woman before? Go and fetch some cushions so that our guest may sit comfortably. Hurry! Shame on you!" I, on the other hand, now stared at this new self-possessed Arqiya ordering her sisters-in-law about—dear Arqiya, now revealing hidden depths that one had little suspected! The girls hastened to obey: a length of new matting was spread out and I was surrounded by cushions, far too many, which I handed round to my hostesses, who at first refused them out of politeness.

"Have you heard the news? Have they told you?" Arqiya nodded her head in the direction of Bu Tahar's house.

"No, what? Tell me!"

"I think I am pregnant. . . at last!" Arqiya sighed proudly and happily. "I *am* lucky; Muh is so kind to me. Look what he has brought back from the *suq* for me: these two silver bracelets!" She shook her wrist and two bright bangles jingled with the others already adorning her arm. Somehow in l-'Ass life was easier and more affluent; the women had time to dress up and the houses were bigger and more comfortable. Yes, Arqiya had made a good marriage; Muhand had chosen well for her.

Hadda was jealous of the new bride and her first pregnancy. "When I was first married my husband gave me presents, too. He even gave me a *gold* bracelet," she boasted. "But now I suspect that he is thinking of another wife, because I have only given him daughters and I don't seem to be able to get pregnant again."

"I had three daughters before I had a son," Maghniya consoled. To join the conversation I remarked that I, too, had two daughters before a son was born. "So don't worry, be patient."

"No, don't worry," echoed Arqiya, "God will provide in his own good time." Then she confided to me: "She nearly died, you know, with the last baby; it took three days to deliver. . . yet they say the first baby is the hardest." Arqiya seemed unafraid of what lay in store for her, for she added brightly, "I hope my first child will be a boy!"

"Indeed yes, *Insha'llah!"*

Maghniya, who had been the longest married of the young wives, turned to me to express her views on married life. It was obviously an opinion that her sister-in-law did not share, for she turned her back on her completely to brook no interruption while she stated to me: "Hadda does not know how lucky she is to only have two children. She has proved she is not barren so she can't be divorced. God is merciful in giving her a rest."

Hadda could not keep silent. "But supposing he does bring another wife. . . I think I'd poison her!" she burst out.

"No, you wouldn't. . . As I was going to say," persisted Maghniya, "Hadda still has her strength and likes her husband working in bed with her. . . you understand?" She looked at me piercingly.

"Yes, I can keep him *that* way!" the impetuous Hadda interrupted again.

". . . As I was *saying*," continued Maghniya pointedly, "when I lost my shyness I thought bed was fun too at first—" she winked at Arqiya, who blushed—"though now with four children and quite enough work, I'm not too sure, as all I want to do is *sleep*! But 'Ali seems more energetic than ever!" Maghniya frowned as she bit delicately at an almond. "I suppose I shall have to get pregnant again or *he* will become suspicious, as the baby is nearly eight months old."

"What have you been doing to prevent your having another baby?" I was curious to know.

"I just push in a pad of cloth soaked in vinegar, and so far it has worked. . . She added: "The method with all the knots is a nuisance and dirty, and I can never remember all the words, anyway!"

Now we were fully launched on The Most Enthralling Subject and the questions were fast, but I was becoming very adept in answering them and building up quite a wide vocabulary in sex and midwifery.

"Is it true that Christian women have their babies in *hospital?*" asked Mimuna, the cousin who had not said a word up till now; she had appeared strangely uninterested in our conversation and just sat there playing with her happy nine-month-old baby, who gurgled and kicked on her lap.

I had to admit that most Christian women had their babies in hospital because it was easier to do so, as I had done. This brought up a further question.

"Did you mother-in-law go with you to deliver them?"

"No," I replied, "there are women specially trained to do that, who know what to do if things go wrong." I added: "Not many women die in labor today, in my country."

"*When* you die is Written and is God's Will, and *nobody* can alter that," said Hadda with conviction. *That* brick wall again, I thought to myself, but I said nothing.

"It must be awful not to have your mother or mother-in-law with you when you most need her. Imagine a strange woman pushing and presssing on your belly!" Maghniya was shocked. In some ways I agreed with her: birth in our society seems to have become so impersonal.

"Too many women die in childbirth in your country," I commented, and hurried on before Hadda could interrupt. "If Hadda had been in hospital, she would not have been three days in labor, as she was, and is now, perhaps, hurt inside. And think, it's a rest for the mother, especially when there are other children. She can spend a whole week in bed with nothing to do but sleep, eat and rest." This brought the house down, as I knew it would.

"A whole week! I couldn't stay in bed a whole week! With this last baby I lay on my mat for only two days, after that I had my share of the work to do."

"Are you *still* not pregnant yet with this husband of yours?" was the eternal question, no matter where I went. This time it came from Arqiya, the most recently married. Having known me when she was single she was concerend for me and my future. I was saved an explanation as Hadda brought round the basin, water and a towel for me to wash my hands prior to eating the midday meal. When Arhma brought in a dish of chicken piled high with vegetables, I felt embarrassed that we had been chatting while she had been doing all the preparing and cooking. Arhma set down the dish in the middle of the low table in front of us, broke up some bread, then sat back on her haunches. "Eat!" she commanded. The younger women moved to the edge of the matting and talked among themselves, while Arqiya poured me a glass of water. I did not want to eat as an honored guest, to be waited on hand and foot as is the custom with visiting strangers. I grabbed Arqiya's hand and said: "Arqiya, please, you must eat with me—aren't we old friends from r-'Attaf? Wasn't I one of the family at the henna ritual?"

"That is so," announced Arhma, who had been at the henna ceremony herself. "Munat is one of the family, though she is a guest also. Eat!"

"Bismillah!" we said as we plunged bits of bread into the savory smelling stew—which was, alas, also submerged beneath an inch of the best and most pungent olive oil.

During a meal no one speaks much, for eating is a serious business. When we had washed our hands again and were digesting with glasses of tea, I told them of our visit to El Hoceima hospital with Muhand's family, and about Rwazna's interview with the doctor—who was a *woman,* I was careful to stress—and the high hopes she now had of being able to bear children after some treatment. Arqiya was particularly happy knowing what misery Rwazna's life had been with her in-laws. And, of course, they were all agog to hear every detail of that trip.

Women from neighboring houses dropped in to have a look at the wife of the *Amirikani* who was visiting in Hammadi's house. They sat around and stared and chatted and giggled while questions about me passed back and forth. When I addressed whem directly, they tittered nervously, much too shy to answer. The story of visiting the woman doctor was discussed in detail, Muhand's famly having been the first from that part of the Rif, probably, to have done such a thing. For the most part I was ignored as they spoke in low voices about *women* doctors and of their own problems; but their main and avid interest was in birth control, a perpetual concern of women.

It was already late afternoon when Arhma appeared again. Now she did so to tell that it was time to leave and that she would escort me to Bu Tahar's house. "Why can't my husband and Muhand walk back with me?" I asked. "They left long ago!" was her carefree answer. I protested that it was not necessary to accompany me, pointing out that the trail was easy to follow from her house to his, but to no avail.

"Young women do not go out alone; it is incorrect. I will walk with you. Come along," she ordered, "it will be dark soon and your husband will want to eat," and so saying, Arhma swathed her head in a towel and walked out of the compound. The younger ladies clustered round the door as we said goodbye to one another.

"Come again soon!" they chorused, and watched me politely as I walked down the path, before retiring behind the door which excluded them from the world.

Arhma, straight as a rod, set off at a guardsman's stride and probably twice as fast, talking loudly over her shoulder, though I understood nothing. Then, realizing I was some way behind, she stopped walking and talking and waited while I breathlessly caught up with her. She smiled, lines crinkling her face.

"I'm sorry, I forgot that you are from the town and have no legs. I will walk slowly as your are unaccustomed to our hills." Although, in her opinion, she dawdled, I still had trouble keeping up with her.

"Are your children with your mother-in-law?" she asked. I puffed that my mother-in-law lived in America and that my children were at school, knowing full well that this barbarous custom of ours would bring forth a flood of scorn.

"Agh! I have heard that foreigners send their children away as soon as they can walk!" I was about to protest this gross exaggeration but Arhma gave me no chance and rushed on: "It is a *very bad custom*; children should be at *home*, not at school where all they learn are bad ways!"

"Perhaps you are right, Khatshi Arhma." (*Khatshi,* as well as being a kinship term meaning "mother's sister," is also a polite form of address to an older woman related matrilaterally to the speaker in any way.)

I went on: "I know it is hard for you to understand, but in the work of today we have to send our children to school to learn from books the things they cannot learn at home." And as a crafty afterthought: "How could the woman doctor help people like Rwazna except by going to school to learn!"

Arhma stopped in her stride as though to consider my words, then: "I don't know about *that,* she is not a *Rifian* woman, but I do know that they are trying to pass a law to force us to send *girls* to school, from five to fourteen years old! It's a scandal! Those are the years a girls learns all about the house and how to be a good wife," she stated indignantly. Then she asked me if I had seen the schoolhouse built in r-'Attaf, which was quite new. I answered that I had. It was a one-room building standing on a promontory of land not far from Muhand's house. It was a forlorn and deserted building and I wondered if it would ever be used.

Arhma was now in full flood on this topic she evidently felt so strongly about: "Boys, perhaps, should learn to read and write. . . however, I wonder, when all that is needed is *this* to sign a paper." She thrust out a thumb saying, "No one can ever copy that!" The old lady spoke with such vehemence that this must have been a subject over which she had argued frequently with those around her, the pros and cons of school and emancipation, for she still had a lot more to say and I listened in silence.

"Boys are of more use herding goats and generally helping their fathers. If all the boys are in school, then who is left to work and run errands, eh?" Her eyes were penetrating and challenged me to defy this logical statement. "As for girls," she argued, "they stay at home learning woman's work until they are married. They don't need to use their thumbs on paper. . . Huh! that is not a woman's concern; her house and family *are*!" I panted along beside her trying to gain breath to speak, knowing full well that whatever I said in remonstration would fall on a closed mind.

"Khatshi Arhma, the world is changing and now everyone has to learn to read and write, and soon girls will have to, too; you won't be able to stop it. That doesn't mean, however, that the girls who go to school are *bad* girls." She shook head head violently. "That is just what Muhand says, and I don't agree," Arhma said heatedly. "He wants to send his daughters to school, but he gets those ideas from your husband. Your husband is a good man, and we all like him, but Muhand must not try to copy *Amirikani* ways, for *this is the Rif* and we are *Rifians*." Arhma marched on, head held high.

"That's not fair, Khatshi Arhma! My husband never tries to influence Muhand in sending his daughters to school or interfere in any way with your customs. All he is doing is to teach Muhand to read and write in Spanish." I was annoyed by her insinuations.

"True, true, Munat, I'm sorry. No, your husband does not interfere." Arhma patted my shoulder. "The trouble is here, among our own men. Those who go to work in El Hoceima, or even as far away as Tangier and Casablanca, come back with these ideas that *everyone* should go to school. I don't like it, as it will lead to bad ways, and while *I* live my daughter's daughters will *not* go to school," she announced categorically. We walked on in silence. There was nothing to say; her views were unchangeable, steeped in tradition.

After a few minutes Arhma fired her next shot: "Since you are not barren, why did your first husband repudiate you?" Oh no! not again! The discussions and speculations I was creating in this feminine world! What would be their reaction if I stated the truth? I wasn't brave enough to do so by saying: "incompatibility, and I ran off with another man." Their verdict would have been straightforward and simple: adultery and flight are avenged by death to both parties; there are *no* extenuating circumstances!

I took the cowardly way out, temporizing again: "In our religion a man is only allowed one wife at a time; he cannot just take another if the present wife is useless and I was not a good, obedient wife and we quarrelled all the time." Arhma looked at me patronizingly: "And he divorced you just for that? How stupid men are! A few good beatings is all a woman needs. I can see that, now that I am old, and I firmly believe in it to keep a marriage good."

Arhma chuckled; she had, no doubt, been a wilful girl and she was certainly a woman with a strong personality and convictions. Only it was hard to visualize the old and gracious Hammadi in the role of wife beater! She stopped in her stride and peered at me closely and announced: "When I was young, I had many beatings! . . . And *you,* in particular, I should think, need beating." We chuckled together, woman to woman, and then Arhma continued: "Take Dhamimund: if Sha'ib (Chu-Chukth) beat her well and often she would become a good wife and would, perhaps, have given him children by now." Arhma snorted. "But Sha'ib is a fool and frightened of her, and scurries here and there doing whatever she tells him." The old woman dropped her voice, though there was no one for miles around. "We don't like her and her head is too full of ideas." What Arhma meant was that Dhamimund did not conform to community ideas of good wifemanship; she spent too much time on herself or organized her day so that she was able to do so.

"Dhamimund is very beautiful, though," I remarked to see her reaction. "Beautiful! Pah! What is beauty if you can't or won't bear children? That woman is *no use*, she's not *solid*. Sha'ib is a fool." She stamped along the path as though she were stamping on Dhamimund herself. Poor Dhamimund! Although she was Rifian, she came from another clan, and it just didn't do to be "different."

Our conversation became sporadic, without further tirades or airing of opinions. Dusk was already falling when we reached the house and the weather seemed to have changed. Winter was creeping in, for an icy wind blew among the pines. Without ceremony, Arhma burst into her brother's guest room and announced unecessarily: "Here we are! *As-salam 'alaykum!"* Then she turned to Dave and said: "Your wife spent the whole afternoon gossiping with young women and they never stopped. But. . . "—and she wagged her finger at Dave—"if you want a good wife, an obedient one, you must be like the Rifians and beat her! Beat her hard!"

"I will, Khatshi Arhma, that is sound advice; I most certainly will. As it is, she is late home and no supper is prepared." Dave pursed his mouth and glared at me in pretended anger, as though contemplating a corrective blow on the spot. "No, no, calm yourself, she is a good girl," Arhma came to my rescue. "I can't stay either," she added to Bu Tahar, but she did gulp down a glass of tea before hurrying off, for it was almost dark and this time one of the young men accompanied *her* back.

That night we wrapped up warmly before making our last calls of nature; there was no hazardous cactus tunnel to cope with, it was just anywhere one liked among the pines—all right at night, but completely lacking privacy during the day. Black, bulbous clouds scudded across a half moon, and we paused to admire the beauty and watched the shadows as they moved over the trees and slipped across the ravines and hills. Had we known this was to be our last visit to l-'Ass, we would have felt melancholy. Instead, we contentedly sniffed the resin-scented air, then scuttled indoors to our snug room and cosy sleeping bags.

13

It Is God's Will — Marriage, Sex and Legends

A heavy frost had crept over the mountains during the night and we awoke to a freezing bedroom. Unlike Dave, I was a coward and wriggled into my clothes inside the sleeping bag, in a hurry to get to the ever-burning fire in the women's quarters: we women had the advantage there, as the guest room had no heating. The men probably considered their heavy *jillabas* sufficient warmth. They were impervious to cold for the most part and often went barefooted even on freezing days.

All the ladies were up when I went to join them, no doubt in search of the fire! Even Dhamimund. Coarse porridge simmered in a mighty cauldron, bubbles popping as the air rose to the surface. Rifian porridge is not as we know it, but is made from whole wheat which has been previously soaked and then simmered in milk and water until it is thick and tender. Salt and pepper is added during cooking, and it can be eaten like that or with honey added. Also an excellent cold-weather brew is the morning coffee: still very sweet, but heavily laced with black pepper; in a few moments even one's toes are glowing.

"*La bas!* Good morning! Sleep well?" we greeted and answered one another.

"Munat, brush my hair for me!" Vain, effervescent Arqiya bounced up to me. As I sat brushing her hair, Hadduma suddenly winced and gasped.

"What is it, what's the matter?" She had gone quite pale.

"Just a pain," she wheezed. "I often get it, but never quite as bad as this." Hadduma bent over with beads of perspiration on her forehead and a bluish tinge round her nostrils.

"Where is the pain? Do you feel dizzy?" Not knowing the word for "dizzy," I rolled my head about and turned up my eyes; Hadduma nodded.

"I often feel sick and the pain is here." She pressed my hand to her midriff. I was worried about her. Could it be her heart? Or diabetes (the national disease, almost), or an ulcer maybe? Rifians gnaw at hot peppers the way rabbits gnaw on carrots. I went in search of Muhand to tell him that his wife seemed pretty sick; he was with Dave so I told him about her pains, which she said she had been having for some time. Dave suggested a visit to the hospital, having broken the ice there once before. However, Muhand was irritated by our concern and was very offhand.

"There's nothing wrong with her, and she is as strong as a mule. Woman trouble, I expect—so why fuss with a doctor?" We said no more; Hadduma's physique was certainly sturdy, so perhaps it was only a passing cramp, though I couldn't banish it from my mind.

Barely had I shut the door to the living room when agonized screams came from the yard, and more screams. We raced outside. Three-year old Fadila rolled in the dust clasping her foot. Hadduma prised the child's hands away and a limp and evil black scorpion fell to the ground; one that had not yet gone into hibernation. 'Aisha ran forward and scooped it into a tin.

"Aiee, aiee, aiee," wailed Hadduma as she rocked her shrieking daughter, her own pain forgotten. "Aiee, she'll die," moaned the others—all except Dhamimund, who ripped off her wool belt and tied a tourniquet about the girl's ankle. Then she rushed up the stairs and rattled back down them with a razor blade.

"Hold her tightly," she ordered me as she grabbed Fadila's foot: with two deft strokes she cut across the double sting. Blood gushed out and Dhamimund squeezed then sucked the wound and spat, repeating this several times. Fadila's cries had brought the men into the compound. I was about to wash the wound and bind it up.

"No!" Dhamimund stopped me. "This will cure the poison. *Never* put water on a scorpion sting!" In the commotion I had not noticed 'Aisha, who had been squashing up the scorpion in a tin; she had added some henna and made it all into a paste, Dhamimund explaining the remedy as she worked: "The poison that is still left in the creature after it has stung acts as an antidote and the henna is a disinfectant." I watched as she smeared the mixture over the bite—interested, but a little squeamish over the lumps of very dead scorpion.

"Now give me the cloth." Dhamimund held out her hand and then bound the poultice firmly into place. The child had a sickly pallor, and seemed almost in a coma. Once again, I could not mind my own business.

"Muhand, we must get Fadila to the hospital and quickly, as she is very ill." Muhand peered at his small daughter lying in Hadduma's lap, while Hadduma rocked back and forth moaning to herself.

"She's all right now; I think she is sleeping."

"She's not asleep, she's unconscious! Look!" I pinched Fadila's arm; there was no response from her as I let it fall back limply. "She'll die! A black scorpion can kill a child as young as that!" Muhand had another close look. "Then it is God's Will," he said fatalistically.

"It is God's Will," everyone echoed.

"Some die young, some die old: *Maktub*—it is written and foreordained." Bu Tahar raised both hands. This attitude was more than I could take: "It is *not* 'written,' and you *can* do something!" Bu Tahar raised his eyebrows at this unseemly outburst, though I spoke in Spanish directly to Muhand. I stormed out to get some support from Dave.

"What on earth is going on? What's happened?" Dave was standing anxiously in the passage when I dashed out, upset and angry. I told him that Fadila had been stung by a scorpion and was unconsious.

"Jeesus!" muttered Dave. I insisted that we had to get to a doctor and get the right serum as it was a large scorpion. To my mind Muhand was just being pigheaded. "'It Is the Will of God' and 'It Is Written' and all that jazz," I continued heatedly, furious at Dave's seeming indifference. Just then both Bu Tahar and Muhand walked in. Bu Tahar spoke directly to Dave: "Explain to your wife that these things have to be left in the hands of God, and we must accept His Will. We have done what *we* can."

Dave nodded briefly, his face expressionless. "It's hard, but you've got to accept it, you can't interfere." But I still thought I could change an age-old attitude: "It is downright laziness because they don't want to walk to r-'Attaf. They think it's not worth it because she's a *girl*, I suppose!" I glared at Muhand.

"No use banging your head against a brick wall," continued Dave placidly. "I know the 'It Is Written' or *'Insha'llah-Maktub'* syndrome is particularly difficult for us Westerners to take, but that's the way it is. In this case, if you stop to think it out, it will take two hours to get to r-'Attaf and to the Land Rover and then another *five* to get to El Hoceima! So you see we really are too far away here from a doctor's help."

Dave was right, of course, when the matter was looked at like that. Then he told the men that we would take a little walk; they just nodded silently, as uncomprehending of my attitude as I was of theirs.

The homemade serum must have been beneficial, as Fadila recovered slowly in her own way. Like a little sick animal, she was laid on an old blanket near the fire and, for the most part, ignored. Her foot was very swollen and blue and she vomited frequently during the first few days; she slept long hours, woke, whimpered and slept again. By the end of the week she was playing again as though nothing had happened.

After the initial novelty, the days in Bu Tahar's house became rather monotonous as my time was spent solely with the women, whereas in Muhand's house I could slip back and forth between the women's courtyard and the guest room, since there was seldom anyone there but Muhand listening indefatigably to his new transistor radio and ready to help Dave with any questions that might crop up. He was a very bright and alert person to talk to anyway, and a rest from the communication struggle.

Why does everything have to turn around sex and babies, I thought irritably as I bounced an unhealthy fat child on my knees. I could hear Dave roaring with laughter at some good joke; the door of the guest room must have been open as the guffaws echoed along the passage. I would much rather have been with him instead of having to mind a baby or knead and slap dough—the only job I was considered capable and strong enough to handle! As it was I had to answer interminable questions:

"Does your husband beat you? Muhand beats Hadduma!"

I was quick to chip in in support of Hadduma: "He beats Khadduj too, because I've heard her crying and him shouting."

"How often does your man sleep with you?" asked one of them, making the usual coarse gestures, and, "Isn't he angry because you haven't given him any children?" and, "Won't he divorce you?" queried another.

"*Why* don't you give him any children?" someone else then demanded, and so on. Fatima, the youngest of the married women, leaned over with her face close to mine and a mischievous smile on her lips and whispered in a voice that everyone was meant to hear: "Do you know how we can tell whether a man will be good in bed with his wife; you know . . . how *big* he is?"

"No! Tell me!"

"Hee, hee, hee!" giggled young Arqiya, digging me in the ribs.

Fatima proceeded to explain: "It is great fun when we are at the spring fetching water and washing clothes and a young man walks past. Sometimes they have to, because the spring is close to the main path to Bulma, way up those mountains." Fatima pointed toward the west. Her eyes darted round merrily while some of the girls laughed with assumed modesty behind their hands. I waited.

"Well, his feet indicate how big 'it' is—you know? What he has hidden in his *sirwal!* So to tease him, especially if we know he is shy, we stare hard at his feet! It never fails to make a man stumble and blush! Ha, ha!" The girls broke into shrieks of mirth.

"Do *you* still play this game, Fatima?" I pretended severity.

"No, no, of course not, now that I am married; that is girls' fun. I have to turn my back when men go by these days, or at least not look."

"And what about you? You are not married," I could not resist asking the most silent and disapproving of the teen-age sisters.

"Of course I don't. Its shameful!" she replied indignantly and, sweeping a braid behind her shoulder, stalked from the room.

"My, my! That's done it!" crowed Ariqiya. "She'll be in a temper for days; but she *does* look, they both do. I've watched them, only they're sly." Arqiya drawled out the word with her eyes screwed up, then pranced round the room, her beads jumping about her neck. "You should see 'Amar n-Muh Akkuh's feet, they are *enormous!* I wonder if I'll be married to him?" Arqiya, in an explosion of laughter, darted outside.

"Really, that girl has no shame," complained Hadduma, more for form's sake than really caring.

"Do Christian women tattoo their faces, hands or bodies?" 'Aisha asked, starting a fresh subject. 'Aisha herself had the standard vertical tramlines with dots on her chin and forehead. However, she held out her hands for me to note the geometrical design that had been drawn across the backs and palms. Then she plucked up Hadduma's skirt so that I could admire the delicate pattern that had been tattooed up the ankle. I remarked how pretty it was, adding that we didn't do anything like that—at least, not women. "Sometimes our men do, though, and in bright colors."

"What! *Men* wear tattoo marks? But that's for women!" shrilled Dhamimund, who had just come in with a tray of bread.

"Not in our country," I told her. "It is usually soldiers or sailors or men who work in the mines"—a labor the women knew about—"who tattoo themselves," adding that it was very painful to do and usually cost a lot of money, and that the patterns were not the same as Rifian ones.

"Show us!" demanded Arqiya, snatching up my notebook and pen from a shelf. So I drew them pictures of birds and flowers and even entwined hearts explaining their significance, as well as one which bore the legend "MOTHER."

"Mother!" Arqiya shrieked. "If a man is big enough to bear the pain of tattooing, he is big enough to do without his mother," was 'Aisha's practical comment.

Hadduma explained to me that girls were tattooed when they were very young, just a few pricks each day. "They scream, but they soon forget." She pointed to Fadila, saying that she didn't even know now that she had a tattoo on her chin. "I don't remember anything about it and I've got patterns all over my legs," said Hadduma, pulling her skirt high to show me. She added wistfully: "The custom is dying out now, and somehow we don't seem to have the time any more; I don't know why." Nonetheless, as Hadduma informed us, "Many older women have patterns tattooed all over them, on their breasts, stomach and even backsides and right down their legs."

"What a wonderful time husbands must have had on their wedding nights, following all those patterns—not that they need a pattern to guide them where they want to get!" 'Aisha burst into unrestrained laughter while trying to teach me the intricacies of cat's cradle. Rifian girls, and sometimes younger married women, play this game as a time-filler. They have brought it to a fine art with many additional finicky and complicated pattern executions. Beyond the initial movements I was all thumbs against her delicate fingers, grimy as they might have been. Occupied in a tricky execution I felt Fatima's eyes boring into me. "There is something we all want to know, in fact we have been talking about it," she said with the frankness of youth.

"*Stuk*! Shut-up!" both 'Aisha and Hadduma snapped. I looked from one to the other. In what had I been found wanting now? I was so inept at practically everything I was given to do.

"It doesn't matter," said Hadduma, irritated by 'Aisha and wanting to be the tactful hostess. But my curiosity was roused and I insisted that they tell me.

"It's this: Why didn't your husband marry a virgin for this first marriage, a young woman like me or 'Aisha? You are not very young, you are not rich and you have no jewelry at all!"

Dhamimund joined the conversation: "Perhaps the family arranged it because it was a good match between the two families, as with Muhand and Hadduma. Hadduma is quite a bit older but she *was* a virgin."

It was time to blow another belief and enlighten them on a further fact of Western life: "When my grandmother was young, parents arranged their children's marriages, but that no longer happens today. People over twenty-one"—this was old in the Rif—"can marry whom they like." The group stared at me in round-eyed wonder. This notion was beyond their conception; it simply was not done.

"You mean you can just marry anyone from *anywhere* and it does not matter?" Incredible as this thought was, Dhamimund was considering it.

"I certainly would not like to marry a stranger," Silent Sister commented. "Nor I!" agreed Sullen Sister.

"It is our custom to get to know the man first and find out how we get along; if we don't like each other we let him go and look for someone else. And not *all* Christian women want to get married."

"Oooh!" both sisters gasped in horror.

"And did you arrange your *first* marriage?" questioned Arqiya.

"That's right—he was *very* handsome!"

"And *you* found your second husband? For yourself?"

"Of course!" I grinned at them as they shook their heads in stunned amazement, wondering if I might not be a "bad" woman. For these tribeswomen, love, as understood in the West, is not common. Mutual respect and companionship is virtually unknown, as is physical self-restraint on the part of the man. For the established woman with a family, the dread of bearing yet another child soon kills all desire for sexual relations and sex just becomes another unavoidable chore.

As we discussed marriage, wife-beating and divorce the door creaked open and Fadhma's wrinkled face peered round it.

"As-salam 'alaykum!"

"Wa 'alaykum as-salam!" we all called back, wondering what the reason was for the old lady's visit. She normally never sat with us in the communal room, though we often saw and talked to her outside as she went about her business. Arqiya was very attentive to her great-aunt. She had already arranged some cushions on the nicest part of the matting and now invited her solicitously toward them.

"Whatever has come over you, Arqiya? I am quite capable of walking unaided, and well you know it! No doubt you've been up to some mischief!" Fadhma's voice was surprisingly firm, as was her step. Only her face showed the decades of toil and weather she had endured.

"I'm sure none of you have been to fetch water yet? No, of course not! Munat is here and there is a lot to talk about." Fadhma's glance twinkled round the room as her daughters-in-law sought excuses for their indolence. "Today I am coming with you. I know all about the things young women talk about, but has anyone of you told Munat of our legends?" The ladies shook their heads; legends had never occurred to them, nor had they to me either.

"Ah! I thought so. Get the water jars and we will go. Come!" She turned to me: "We have no pots to carry, we will go ahead." The energy of the elderly woman put me to shame; she was already striding out of the door.

It was a walk of about a mile to the spring along a narrow path with a high bank on one side and on the other the ground fell away to olive trees and plots of land. In some of them men were ploughing slowly and laboriously because it was so steep. They called commands to their beasts when it was the moment to turn, almost on the proverbial dime, and churn up the next furrow with the handmade wooden plow.

The pool, fed by the spring to which I had walked many times before, was sheltered in a rocky alcove with a beautiful little waterfall that tumbled between boulders and ferns to form a small stream on the other side of the path. Fadhma pointed to the gurgling water: "This is a miraculous spring; today, because it is cold, the water is tepid. Feel it." I did, and she was right. "In summer," she continued, "it is always cool, clear and sparkling. Look up, there is the source of the spring." Fadhma pointed to about fifty feet above our heads where there were immense creeper-strewn rocks down which one could hear the water dribbling and dripping.

"It's beautiful here, isn't it? Cool in summer and shady, and warm and sheltered in winter." Fadhma sat down, patting a place for me to sit beside her while she told her tales: "The story goes that once, long ago, one of the *shurfa*"—descendants of the Prophet Muhammad—"or saints of the holy lineage of Sidi Hand u-Musa, had traveled far and long over the barren mountains till he came to these huge boulders and trees that gave such wonderful shade, and beneath them he rested." Fadhma looked around her as I did. The others had caught up with us and were idly splashing in the stream. They were bored by the story they knew so well; the past did not interest them greatly. "So what!" their collective expressions conveyed, except for Hadduma, who seemed ill and tired as she sat listlessly on a stone. Ignoring the others, Fadhma proceeded:

"So there he was, hot, thirsty and tired. Above all thirsty—he'd walked for miles without a drop to drink." Fadhma spoke with such conviction that she might have trudged those barren mountains herself.

"While debating how much further he could go, he tapped on the ground with his staff and, to his astonishment, out gushed cool, clear water, right there at his feet. That water has continued to flow ever since."

"This is so, and it is the gift of God," Hadduma called across to us. "Indeed, ever-flowing water is the gift of God," echoed 'Aisha piously.

"It tastes very sweet and is so soft," I added, for fear that my silence might be misconstrued as scepticism. While the water jars were being filled we sat on a grassy mound facing down the stream toward sheer rock cliff at least two hundred feet high. The black granite surface gleamed, smooth and slippery. Ignoring the babble and chatter I became absorbed in a fantasy: if I had to escape some horror or be a heroine could I scale that formidable cliff To Save My Virtue? Though I knew I could not and that Virtue would be lost I stared more closely and sought for hand or foot holds. Nothing. It was like glass. A tugging at my sleeve brought me back to the spring.

"What do you see, Munat?" Fadhma peered at me anxiously.

"Why, nothing! I was just noticing that, there, the cliff is sheer and no trees grow anywhere, while on this side it is mossy, shady and green." I glanced at the other women, who stared at me without expression, almost hostile. Suddenly I felt like an outsider; the door was closed, despite all the hospitality and conviviality we had shared.

"Are you *sure* you saw nothing?" Hadduma looked suspicious.

"Of course not!" What was I expected to see? Admittedly the rock was very forbidding and looked out of place in the rest of the lushness. Perhaps there had been an accident there and the ghost still haunted the cliff. Speculations were brought to an end by Fadhma, who had not shut me out of her world.

"I'll tell you. There is a legend about the cliff—aha!" Fadhma held my arm in a strong grip. "Long ago in the days when miracles and other equally amazing things happened, there were men who walked along this very path and some claimed that they saw a horse and rider gallop *up* the cliff. Not everyone had the gift to see this vision for it foretold that something extraordinary or dreadful would happen." Fadhma paused, then resumed: "Once there was a great famine and the horse and rider were seen then; and then just before Independence they were seen again."

"Oh? By whom?" I tried not to sound doubting.

"Just a passer-by." Fadhma waved her hand airily while I studied the perpendicular granite. "Well, *I* haven't seen anything!" I said firmly.

"Of course you haven't! Nobody we *know* has ever seen the horseman; it is always somebody else." 'Aisha placatingly patted my knee.

"Anyway, it's only the *very* old and saintly men who claim to have seen him, and there is no one around like that now!" Arqiya, of the up-and-coming generation, interested only in the here and now, tossed a stone in the air, twirled about and headed off home balancing a toddler on her hip.

Nevertheless, Fadhma believed firmly in the saints, their visions and activities. She swept her arm out toward the hills: "*Everybody* knows that saints and very holy men flew invisibly to Mecca and back *the same day* from these very peaks, the peaks of the Jbil Hmam!" She pursed her lips and nodded her head up and down as though following a bouncing ball, while I stared with doubting eyes at the mountaintops, trying to calculate how many thousand miles a saint would have to fly and how fast on a round trip from the Rif to Mecca in the same day. For he would have had to do so through the agency of *baraka*, the miraculous God-given power which presumed and guaranteed the gifts of instant flight and the invisibility of the flyer, as well as the ability of horsemen to ride up and scale perpendicular cliffsides.

14

Birth and Baby Care

"I know now, and for sure," 'Aisha said somberly as I entered the compound to begin the daily round with its inmates.

"What do you know for sure?" I asked as I closed the door.

"'Aisha is pregnant again." Fatima wiped away tears with the back of her hand. Fatima was crying and 'Aisha was looking equally miserable over her prospective pregnancy. Evidently the reality did not conform to the ideal—the ideal being a baby almost every year. . . from the man's viewpoint! This would be 'Aisha's fourth baby.

"Is that so dreadful, 'Aisha? Your husband must be very proud of you, surely?"

"I haven't told him yet, though I've suspected it for some weeks." She lowered her voice: "You see, I've been thinking about going to the midwife to help me get rid of it." "Aiee!" wailed Fatima, wringing her hands, as well she might.

"Oh, don't do that!" I gasped involuntarily, imagining some filthy woman poking and bungling around with 'Aisha, and quite possibly causing her death through infection. Though such acts are *haram* (forbidden), desperate women do resort to them, but it is very difficult in a small community to keep the word from getting around. There are no medically trained midwives in the Rif, only old women, experienced in childbearing (and superstitions), though past the age themselves. Nothing is known about sterilization, and heaven help the unfortunate woman if there are complications; usually she dies after days of agony.

"But what else can she *do*? She had such an awful time the last time!" moaned Fatima, who was very close to her sister.

"I suffer so terribly with each birth, and each time it's worse. I nearly died the last time," repeated 'Aisha, "I lost so much blood with all the pulling and pushing. I'm *afraid* to go through it all again! Look how weak and small Muhammad is."

This was true, for none of 'Aisha's children looked healthy. Muhammad was always crying in a thin, sickly way, though she fed and nursed him constantly, and the others had permanently runny noses or sore eyes. What could I say to boost her morale? A difficult birth must be torture; no wonder 'Aisha was frightened. I was quite inadequate to advise her on this insoluble female dilemma.

"Have you yourself tried anything to get rid of it? Pomegranate seeds? Hot pennyroyal tea?" I asked in an attempt to cheer her up.

"I've tried that, and drinking the bitter water from the pomegranate peel, as well as eating causarine seeds; but they are poisonous and it only made me sick. I've even tried lifting heavy pots of water up and down! But it is no good!" 'Aisha now began to sob desperately.

"There, there, God is merciful, it may not be so bad this time," said Hadduma to console 'Aisha, who was her particular friend. She looked to me to put forward a suggestion. Those I had mentioned, 'Aisha had already tried; all that remained was the old wives' tale of castor oil, though there was none available. Possibly their pungent olive oil would have the same effect if taken in large quantities.

I put it forward as the only thing I could think of: "Have you tried drinking the very strongest and greenest oil you have? Some women in my country try this; you have to take it in the morning before you eat or drink anything else. And take it very hot. Sometimes it works, but not often!"

"Ugh!" choked Arqiya, unfeelingly, in mock sickness, holding a hand over her mouth.

"If you can get it down, drink it several days running; it might help."

"Anything! Anything! If it will help get rid of it," cried 'Aisha in despair. The thought of her coming ordeal was too awful to contemplate.

I warned: "It will make you feel very ill; you'll spend most of your time behind the trees and. . ."

"She won't mind losing her intestines if she can lose the baby too!" Arqiya interrupted again, callously.

"It is only a suggestion now, so don't be angry with me if it doesn't work and you only feel ill." I turned to Fatima and asked her if she felt nervous about the coming birth of her own baby. Birth among traditional tribal women is not a private affair, and she had already seen the repeated sufferings of her sister.

"Why be afraid?" Fatima replied, a little surprised by such a question. "We are meant to bear children and Allah gives us the strength to bear the pain, so His Will must be accepted, come what may. Hadduma has babies as easily as hens lay eggs, but for 'Aisha. . . God has willed it differently." Fatima looked forward to the day when she hoped that her husband could proudly fly a white flag from the roof of the house to show that a boy had been born into the family. Fatima could not help the time to pass quicker by making baby clothes and gathering together a layette. Rural babies do not have special clothes; they are put into whatever is available. To begin with, they are rolled tightly in a cloth and kept covered and later they are dressed in hand-me-downs and tuck-me-ups, or they go around seminaked, whatever the weather.

Everyone had something to say about how Rifian women handled birth. Hadduma stirred the cauldron that perpetually simmered among the ashes. It contained either porridge or stew, according to the hour of the day. The ladies gathered closer; they had a new listener to talk to on their ever-absorbing topic of birth, a listener who wanted to hear all about such a mundane occurrence. Hadduma's sad eyes looked into mine and all at once, in her expression, I saw Hmid, her eldest son. From her came his innate understanding and sympathy for others less fortunate and more apt to make mistakes, as I did in those early days. (Indeed, in their view, I was still pretty inept as a housewife right up until the end of our fieldwork.)

As the oldest of the wives and the most experienced in childbirth Hadduma began, and she spoke slowly, with Fadila snuggled in her lap:

"When labor starts the woman sends for two of her female relatives, or elderly women who have borne children, and who then act as midwives. Throughout her labor she is given nothing to eat or drink. It is considered bad luck should the woman defecate during labor pains. The midwife, who is often the girl's mother, ties a rope to a beam for her to pull on. As the pain increases, she pulls harder on the rope; it helps the baby to come down. Understand?"

I nodded. "What do you do if things go wrong and the baby is not coming the way it should?"

"What *can* one do? If the child is stuck the midwife tries to pull it from the mother's body, leg by leg, or arm by arm."

"As happened to me once while someone knelt on my stomach," 'Aisha interrupted to say No wonder she was afraid!

Hadduma resumed: "However, when the birth takes days, the mother usually dies and so does the child." 'Aisha was silent as she thought of her last ordeal.

"As the moment draws near," continued Hadduma, "one of the midwives holds the girl's knees and, at the moment of birth, her mother or mother-in-law clasps her firmly round the waist with one arm to help push out the baby. With the other hand she presses hard on the anus so that the child does not appear from there." Hurriedly I turned a laugh into a cough. Hadduma was serious and intent on her information.

"To be born like that is shameful and bad luck, too," joined in Dhamimund.

"And what do *you* know about it?" spat 'Aisha acidly.

"Let's not quarrel," interposed Hadduma. "Munat wants to learn how we do things. Then 'Aisha took up the tale: "If it is a boy, the midwife cuts the cord with scissors. If it is a girl, it is severed with a sickle so that next time the mother will be lucky and bear a son. The woman then rubs a little blood on the mother's cheeks in order to get her strength back."

As in most non-literate or illiterate societies, the placenta plays an important role in birth, I learned. It is taken by one of the midwives some distance from the house and buried deeply so that it will not be dug up and eaten by dogs, as this would render the woman barren.

Whatever may have been the duration of the woman's labor, midwives are paid two duros (one shilling or ten cents, in 1965). On the seventh day, the name-giving day, they are rewarded with a sheep or goat's head to flavor the couscous.

Birth is a great event and every female member of the household, including young children, are present and crowded into the delivery room. They help to run errands, make tea, push or pull on the expectant mother's anatomy. Men, and boys over the nursing stage (about two years old), are rigidly excluded, even from the central courtyard.

The women boil basil, as an astringent herb, and use the water to mix up a paste of henna and earth. They spread this on a piece of thin cloth and apply it to the vagina to arrest bleeding and prevent infection. What with goats, mules and chickens roaming freely, tetanus must be rife. For the tough tribeswomen birth is certainly a hazard; death must be a happy release from utter torture if things go wrong.

"If labor is very protracted and if the mother is not too near death, is she still given *nothing*?" I asked. "Not even a little drop of sweet tea to sustain her?"

"No, nothing! It is bad luck," was Hadduma's instant reply. She continued: "The mother has a little camomile tea to drink when it is all over and she is not too exhausted, which helps the milk to come in and flow.

"Who washes the baby? The midwives?" was my next question.

"Wash the baby?" the group cried, horrified. All eyes riveted upon me, angry and aghast that, after all our talks, I could still ask such an ignorant question.

"A baby is *never* washed for the first year," Fatima informed me in an uncharacteristically prim voice.

"I'm sorry, I didn't know; we consider the first wash very important. The baby is bathed as soon as it is born, especially the eyes. We wash them in a very special mixture like water—to keep away the Evil Eye," I added for good measure. This was met with disapproving silence. I hastened to say: "But please continue. I want to learn about *your* customs; I'm not finding fault." 'Aisha eyed me speculatively for a moment, then accepted my apology.

"Yes, all right. Your customs are different and for the most part not good. However. . . Well, after a year the mother can give the baby a bath, but even after that, not more than two or three a *year*, mind you, because bathing is weakening. The baby, of course, stays in the room in which it was born for two weeks and during the first week it is never allowed to see daylight. It is wrapped up and kept covered all the time by a cloth. Evil spirits are always around just waiting for the chance to cast a bad spell."

Fatima chipped in with her own knowledge: "A child should never be out in strong daylight when it is very young, or shown to too many women"—here she glanced at Dhamimund, who started back defiantly—"as one of them might be jealous and work a spell for the baby to die." 'Aisha leaned forward to finger baby Muhammad's shift and added: "Naturally we wash the *clothes* and *cloths* constantly, but washing the *baby* would wash away its strength; then it would just get sick and die. The Evil Eye attacks babies most of all." 'Aisha sighed enormously at the unjustness of fate. I remained silent, not daring to comment.

It might be added that sexual intercourse is permitted during pregnancy, but is strictly taboo and shameful for six weeks (forty days) after birth. This is a Qur'anic injunction which is rigidly adhered to.

"One thing I forgot to tell you," said 'Aisha as we were assembling the water jars and washing. "Should two women who are living in the same house give birth on the same day, they are careful to avoid each other for the next forty days. If they have the misfortune to meet, it is certain one or the other of the mothers or babies will sicken and die." When I repeated to the women of l-'Ass that Christian women rested and stayed in bed for at least a week after their babies were born, they could not believe such indulgence.

"How wonderful!" exclaimed 'Aisha, "especially as she had had a bad time and needs a rest."

"Yes," echoed Hadduma wistfully, adding that within a week of having her last baby she had been up and trundling back and forth with wood on her back and Fadila at her breast. "And talking of wood," said Hadduma, "I'd better go and collect some." So saying she got up reluctantly to resume her work.

"As I have no children yet, I want to stay in bed for a week, like a foreign woman," joked Fatima. "But what would be the use of that as Mimun wouldn't be able to stay in bed with me!" She laughed merrily as she hoisted the water jar to her back, not giving it a second thought that heavy weights might be bad for her, and nor did anyone else. Women stayed in harness until they were in labor.

So we set off to the spring that I so enjoyed, Dhamimund leading the way, walking proudly adorned with her glinting jewelry while I moved along somewhere in the middle minding the small children. I was silent, humbled and lost in thought over the ordeal that Rifian tribeswomen went through to bring forth a child, with the continual dread that, after all, it might only be a daughter, while we Western women had such pampered pregnancies and births.

Their beliefs were not for me to challenge. As of the mid-1960s clinics with Moroccan nurses and doctors of both sexes were gradually infiltrating into the remoter parts of the country. Nonetheless it may be sometime yet before country and tribal women have the courage to flaunt the beliefs and customs of generations in favor of Western ways, especially when it comes to beliefs and practices connected with childbearing, which are still strongly anchored in tradition.

15

Death . . . and Farewell

I had no premonition that morning that the day would be filled with drama and sorrow. As I helped Hadduma sift the flour she looked unhappy and stared absent-mindedly into space.

"What's the matter, Hadduma? You look sad."

"Can't you stay with us a little longer? Ask your husband," she pleaded. An anxious expression puckered her forehead and her large black eyes were filled with unhappiness. My heart went out to this simple, kind and lonely woman. I guessed her unhappiness to be all tied up with Muhand and his inconsideration of her feelings. Hadduma now abandoned all attempt at pounding grain. She just wanted to talk:

"I have given him five children—perhaps there will be six if God wills—so I should be glad that he still comes to see me, however rarely it happens. It is lonely for me, in spite of my children, and Hmid is a good and kind son. But now that he is growing up he has to be where his father is. All the other women have their men to take care of, but I have no one." A great shuddering sigh escaped her as she continued almost in a whisper: "I know he doesn't care for me—I am old." Hadduma was at most thirty-five, probably younger. The beginning of our heart-to-heart was interrupted by the ladies taking up their morning tasks and, in particular, by Dhamimund clattering down the stairs. This time she was not resplendent in her jewelry. Only her eyes sparkled, and in anger.

"Good morning, Dhamimund! To what do we owe the honor of this early visit?" asked Fatima facetiously.

"You've been listening to my radio again, using up the batteries!" she accused the room in general. No one said a word, because we had in fact been listening to Egyptian music with Arqiya undulating to its rhythm by the door as she kept guard to warn us when Dhamimund hove into sight with her bundle of wood.

"If you were generous, and left the radio down here for all of us to listen to, then we would even share the price of the battery," retorted 'Aisha slyly. Dhamimund looked thunderous—and over such a petty matter.

"No doubt Muhand borrowed it," lied Fatima blatantly. We all knew that Muhand never moved without his own new toy, so Dhamimund was just spoiling for a fight and as she made her bread she began to taunt Hadduma.

"So Munat and her husband are leaving soon and your man is going back to his other prettier wife? She knows how to give him a good time in bed, I bet!" Dhamimund laughed cruelly and added: "Nor does he call you to spend a little time with him in the afternoon, I've noticed. You are old and ugly, but at *least* you could wear nicer clothes for him when he *is* here, eh?"

This was too much; how *could* Dhamimund be so nasty? I wanted to stick up for Hadduma, then remembered in time Dave's admonition: "Do not take sides, remain impartial." How impossible! Meanwhile Hadduma said nothing. She could not; and Dhamimund did not see the tear that rolled down her cheek and splashed on to Fadila's spoon as she fed her daughter gruel. But 'Aisha did, and Fatima too.

"And where does *your* husband go after lunch, may I ask? Back to the fields! Your pretty dresses don't lure him to call you, *I've* noticed too!" shouted 'Aisha in defense of her friend." Ha! Ha! Ha!" she laughed raucously; this must have been an old quarrel, for I had been quite forgotten.

"You are nothing more than donkeys, all of you, obedient to your husbands. None of them have been further than El Hoceima, while *mine* has traveled to Algeria and worked there as *top* man on an immense farm. He also knows the *huge* city of Oujda intimately!" screamed Dhamimund in gross exaggeration of that sleazy, second-rate provincial capital and frontier town. It was true that Chu-Chukth had worked in Algeria and, with his Rifian honesty and intelligence, had soon become foreman of the farm workers.

Fatima now joined in the fray. She placed a hand on her hip boastfully displaying her swollen belly and said in a primly icy voice: "I have been married less than a year and already I am giving my husband a child. *You* are barren and can give him nothing! Sha'ib works hard all day to sell what he grows but he doesn't work on you at nights any more. I *know*, because I sleep under your room and I don't hear the boards banging and creaking any more!"

I burst out laughing at this intimate revelation, but quickly stopped, as in her fury Dhamimund hurled a tin plate at Fatima with the remains of the flour she had measured out still in it. This was more than Fatima could bear and she hurled herself on Dhamimund, retaliating with some hefty kicks. 'Aisha and I jumped up to separate the fighting cats before Dhamimund could land a blow that might hurt Fatima.

"Pregnant *donkey,*" Dhamimund hissed as she swirled out of the door with her bread toward the ovens. Fatima and 'Aisha proceeded to clean up the room, whispering to each other, while Hadduma said not a word. She just sat there, all hunched up, nursing the hurt that would take long to heal. I squeezed her shoulder, then ladled out some breakfast for Dave.

When I took him his barley porridge, which we had taken to eating against the cold, the men themselves appeared ill-humored. Mimun, Fatima's husband, was having an argument with Muhand and they were both shouting and Bu Tahar was laying down the law and banging his stick on the table. Dave was having his own private, ineffectual and perpetual quarrel with the flies (despite the cold weather): "*Goddamn* these flies!" he muttered and bashed at them uselessly as they dive-bombed his almost bald head, which made a perfect landing strip. Muhand paused in his argument to address me: "I suppose Dhamimund is being insulting and Hadduma weepy because I'm off soon? And the rest of them screeching and spitting and scratching like cats—it always happens!" Muhand snorted in contempt of a house full of women and continued his grumble: "Thank God we *are* going! At least I'll be home and master again in my own house where no one can interfere." Though he now spoke in Spanish, he glanced irritably at his uncle.

"Haven't you learned to cook barley properly yet, Rifian style? This is just horrible," Dave said to me in disgust as he pushed his plate away. I retorted that *I* hadn't cooked it, Hadduma had, and I told him that she was all upset and that all the marrieds were having a screaming fight. "It's a lovely morning in there, I can tell you!" And so saying I picked up his almost full bowl and left him unsympathetically to the flies.

All the women had vanished to their separate quarters except for Hadduma. Arqiya, at least, was cheerful and humming and bouncing 'Aisha's youngest baby to sleep on her back.

"Let's go to the spring ahead of the others and I'll help you with your washing," I suggested to Hadduma, who was still weepy. There was no sign of the other children when usually the house was overflowing with them. Only Fadila came along and she toddled ahead of us. It was a slow, silent walk and when we got there we sat on a rock that the sun was just beginning to warm and watched the minnows darting through the amber water.

"Don't be unhappy, Hadduma." I took her work-coarsened hand. "You must not believe all that Dhamimund says. Khadduj has had three children very quickly and the last one was stillborn. She is often sulky and complains that she feels sick and has headaches." I wanted to cheer up Hadduma without revealing the "inside story" of another household. "Muhand keeps threatening he'll find another wife, and I've often heard him say that l-'Ass is the only place where he has any peace, and I think that is true."

"Perhaps," sighed Hadduma, staring into the water. Then she spoke *at* me rather than to me, almost in a trance, her thoughts tumbling out:

"Muhand was only fifteen and I was already twenty when we were married. I have never been beautiful and he has never desired me. The reason our parents arranged the marriage was because our lineages were of equally good standing and because of property considerations." Hadduma blinked reminiscently, as though her life were pictured in the pool at her feet, and continued:

"The night we consummated the wedding, he knew nothing, only what every child learns from animals and sharing his parents' room. I knew nothing either. I was a virgin. . . naturally. Yet to him I was an old woman who *should* have known something!" A sob caught her voice.

"And he beat me. It wasn't like two young people learning, happy to learn together. Because I was older it seemed silly to him that I was shy and frightened; that's how Muhand felt about me that first night. He was angry. He took me because he had to—to be a man; not because he wanted me." Hadduma heaved another quivering sigh. Having seen Muhand angry, I could well imagine how rough he must have been.

"Poor Hadduma. . ." I started to say, sighing unhappily with her myself. But she wanted no interruptions and resumed:

"I became pregnant almost at once and Muhand strutted around, pleased to have proved his manhood at such an early age; and I was proud too. I was lucky and had an easy labor and birth for a first child." Hadduma looked up and now her eyes shone as she remembered new motherhood.

"I was so happy because my baby was a boy. The white flag was flown from the house and Muhand was so proud at being the father of a son; he was a *man* and not yet sixteen! Proud, too, that he had a son to carry on the inheritance. Such feasting there was at the name-giving! Nothing was too much work or expense." Hadduma laughed a young laugh at the memory of it and hurried on with her tale.

"For a short time we were happy together. It was not long, though, before I understood that all he wanted from me was to bear children. Already he was looking round for another, younger, prettier girl. I could do nothing right—except produce children. My mother-in-law [Arhimu] is a very kind woman and gentle. She was very understanding. However, out of five children, I gave him three sons." Hadduma proudly pushed back her shoulders and smiled her exquisite smile.

"What happened to the second wife, Hadduma?" Her face closed and her tone was wary as she replied: "She was fourteen and Muhand had seen her at the spring between here and r-'Attaf while she was fetching water with other women. He was crazy to marry her, and in time it was arranged. It was a good match for the girl because, as you know, Muhand belongs to a powerful and respected family." Hadduma dropped a stone into the clear water, scattering the minnows. "Fadhma, the new wife, had her quarters here in the house and I was happy in my home in r-'Attaf where he left me alone during my third pregnancy." What had been those blighted hopes, I wondered. Far off we heard Dhamimund calling petulantly to Fatima to hurry; they were on their way here and I wanted to hear about the second wife. Muhand had told Dave many a time that she practiced sorcery and had tried to poison him; of this he was firmly convinced.

Hadduma picked up her tale: "Anyway, soon after Arqiya was born, Muhand became strange; and though he came back to me, to my rooms, he wouldn't sleep with me and he spent a lot of time with his mother. He was very quiet, often angry. He said that Fadhma was a witch and was trying to poison him and make him impotent. Then Muhand became sick and started vomiting and so he was convinced of this. I think he went to see a *fqih* [Qur'anic teacher] for a cure and then he divorced her. He became better quite quickly and soon after he married Khadduj and I was moved up here."

I wanted to know more. "What did Fadhma actually *do* to Muhand?" I persisted. Most women know something of sorcery but only a few practice it. However, Hadduma closed up; she was not going to tell me and she shied away from the question.

"I don't know, and I didn't want to get involved. Also I began to feel sick myself then too, and suspected Fadhma of casting a spell on me. I went secretly to an old lady who works charms; she gave me one that drove away any evil that Fadhma might have invoked. It is only in the last year or so that I have been getting these sharp pains which get worse and worse." I nodded, remembering how sick Hadduma had looked and the futility of expecting Muhand to do anything about it.

"I always feel tired now, but that's woman's lot." Hadduma stood up. "I will just fill the water jar and we will leave the washing until tomorrow, as I don't want to be near Dhamimund at the moment," she whispered as the women approached, all smiles once more.

"Aren't you going to stay here with us, Munat?" asked Fatima as I was picking up the bundle of washing. I mumbled vaguely that I would go back with Hadduma; if we were leaving, there were things I had to pack up.

"If I find Dave has gone out with Muhand somewhere," I told them, "then I'll come back; the water is almost warm enough to wash my hair." Leaving the women to their own washing, I walked on ahead of Hadduma with Fadila clinging to my hand and skipping over stones. Hadduma plodded slowly along, bent under the weight of the jar. We had walked about half a mile, Fadila and I playing football along the path with a pebble, when I heard a gasp.

"Oooh!" There was a groan and a heavy thud. I looked back. Hadduma was crouched forward on the ground; the stopper of the jar had jolted loose and water sloshed out over her and down the path.

As I ran back she collapsed, face forward on the path; water now poured over her, drenching everything. Hurriedly, my hands shaking, I tugged the ropes off her shoulders and partly heaved and partly rolled the heavy jar off her back. I tried to sit her up, but she was too heavy, and all I could do was roll her onto her back and prop her against the bundle of washing.

Hadduma's face had gone completely gray and blotchy and she was gasping for breath and tearing at her dress, apparently unaware of her surroundings. Fadila stood close by, staring and uncomprehending.

"Go to the house!" I urged her. "Call Baba—*go,* go *quickly*!" Fadila toddled off uncertainly, looking back over her shoulder. "GO! Hurry!" I shouted, and threw a small stone at her the way I noticed the women did when they wanted their children to obey at once. Fadila started to run, insecurely. "Hurry!" I called again.

What a frantic dilemma: should I leave Hadduma and race back to the spring for help, or sit with her? "Oy! Oy!" I began to shout in the hope that someone in a field might hear me. "FATIMA!" Surely the women at the spring could hear.

Hadduma had stopped gasping; I peered at her closely. Was she better? Her face was a terrible color and her hands quite bloodless. I loosened her belt, the only piece of restrictive clothing she wore, and dabbed water on her forehead and cheeks, then held her hand. Slowly her eyes opened. "I am dying," she panted the words.

"Ssh, you'll be all right in a minute, just keep quiet," I tried to soothe her. Again she clawed at her dress, breathless once more. Perhaps it was a heart attack and I hadn't the faintest idea of what to do. Massage over the heart to keep it pumping? I massaged desperately. Her grip tightened on my hand and she looked deeply at me, earnestly trying to speak.

"Ssh, quiet," I murmured and continued massaging her heart and as I did kept repeating out loud "*Bismillah! Bismillah*!" to calm Hadduma and to ward off the evil spirits which always lurk around disasters. She tugged at my hand and I leaned close to hear. "Make them. . . make them. . ." She paused and struggled for breath, but whatever she wanted to say was too much of an effort. Hadduma's eyes closed again, but she was breathing, rapid shallow gasps. Probably only a few minutes had gone by, but it seemed an eternity. I *must* get help and ran a few yards up the path and round a bend and could hear the women's voices. Someone laughed. "Aaah FATIMA! AAAH Fatima!" I yelled. The voices stopped and there was an answering shout. (Prefacing a name when calling urgently with "aaah!" gets instant attention and is always heard.)

"Hurry! Hurry here! Hadduma's sick!" Then I ran back. It could only have been seconds when 'Aisha and Arqiya raced round the corner and knelt beside Hadduma's limp body.

"Help me to sit her up," I panted. We half propped her against the bank. Fatima and Dhamimund, who had now come running up, stared at Hadduma in stunned shock. "*Bismillah!*" they said, recovering themselves.

"Run for the men!" 'Aisha gave Arqiya a shove and the girl bolted off. 'Aisha stroked Hadduma's brow as her eyes fluttered and she lay gasping. Then bending over her she began to murmur a prayer which she repeated over and over, and Hadduma visibly relaxed, comforted. I felt her hands and legs and she was very cold, so we draped the still unwashed clothes about her and wrapped her feet in a shirt. Where *were* the men? What was the delay? Suddenly Hadduma opened her mouth in one big gasp then sank, inert, against the bank.

"She's dead! Aiee, aiee, aiee! She's dead!" wailed 'Aisha. "May her soul rest in peace!" Then she broke into a torrent of weeping. I stared, silent in shock. Once the awful truth had hit us there were long lamentations, "Aiee! Aiee! Aiee! Aiee!" without pause. I wept myself; Hadduma's unhappy life had come to an abrupt end. My tears were for Hmid, too, who adored his mother.

The wailing forewarned the men of what they could expect as they came up the path at a run followed by Arqiya, old Fadhma, round-eyed children and toddlers with Dave close behind. His face paled as he stared at Hadduma's inert form; then he looked at me shocked and enquiring.

"We were coming back with the water; there had been a quarrel earlier and she was tired—it must have been a heart attack." Dave nodded, bewildered. "You remember she complained of pains the other day? It all happened so quickly, though it seemed hours before anyone got to us. Poor Hadduma! She had such an unhappy life!" I wept again, then mopped my eyes and wiped my nose with the hem of my skirt, uncaring whether Dave had a handkerchief or not. He put a comforting arm around me. "In that case, God was kind to her and it is a happy release; she went quickly."

In turns Muhand and Chu-Chukth carried Hadduma back to the house, with the women in the rear already keening the death wail.

Like wildfire the news spread and women, as well as men, flocked to cry and mourn with the family. Those from r-'Attaf came up, with the exception of Khadduj, and Hmid was wild with grief. My heart ached to see him; his eyes, usually so eager and bright, were now filled with tears. He pushed through the cluster of women and flung himself on his mother, bursting into despairing sobs. Tenderly Arhimu, his grandmother, picked him up and held him close.

"It is God's Will; it is Written; it is God's Will, may her soul rest in Paradise," Arhimu repeated over and over softly to comfort the weeping boy. I had no way of showing my sympathy except by gentle pats on his shoulder. With a heart-rending wail he tore himself away from his grandmother and rushed outside; it was not until after the funeral that any of his relatives missed him.

According to Muslim practice, if a person dies during the day all haste is made to bury the body before sunset of the same day; and should one die during the night the funeral takes place early the following morning.

The men carried Hadduma to the communal room and laid her on a length of matting that had been spread in a corner cleared for her. The other women and I seated ourselves at the furthest corner of the room while Arhma, Arhimu and Fadhma prepared the body for burial. It was the elderly women who carried out the rituals of death. Water had been heating outside the house, so that the mounting steam, symbolizing the soul, could rise freely to the heavens. After a while the cauldron was brought in and Arhimu, who was Hadduma's mother-in-law, and Fadhma began to wash the corpse from head to foot including the hair. This was carefully combed out and scented and then smoothed and braided round her head.

Meanwhile, Arhma pounded up in a mortar cloves, dried button roses that have a particularly sweet scent, and dried myrtle. Into this she sprinkled some sinbal, an incense resembling creamy pebbles which, when burned or crushed, releases a pungent aroma. Arhma stirred this powdered mixture into a large basin of henna.

The young women, sitting with me at the end of the row, rocked back and forth, keening and crying and flinging their skirts over their heads. So as not to appear conspicuous, I emulated them in their actions. It was an eerie feeling being right in the midst of their keening, and my flesh popped out in goose pimples. Up and down moaned the voices:

"WoooOH oo WHOOoo! Wiri! Wiri!" When one woman paused another took it up. 'Aisha's grief was genuine, and Fatima's too, I think; although with the others it was more the traditional formality of external observances of grief. I was still stunned by Hadduma's collapse and felt quite dizzy with the low, perpetual rocking back and forth and awed by the accompanying ritual.

Sorrowfully the old ladies began to smear the henna down Hadduma's arms and hands and over her entire body including the soles of her feet. All that was left clear was her face. More perfume, an eau de cologne of sorts, was now sprinkled over the corpse. The body was then slipped into a pair of long, white baggy paints and a short white shift with extra long sleeves.

Fadhma opened a wooden chest with a key that hung on a cord from her waist and delved into its mysterious depths. She brought forth a special wooden needle almost as long as a skewer. With it she sewed up the sleeves of the shirt and the legs of the pants, thereby concealing both hands and feet. Arhimu swathed a white turban round Hadduma's head and face, leaving only her eyes, nose and mouth visible.

The bier that had been hurriedly constructed was brought to the door and Hadduma's body was lifted onto it by the male residents of the community, who always take turns acting as pallbearers.

Fatima had covered my head with a towel and now we all got up and, one by one, walked past the bier either touching Hadduma's covered hand or her head. Then we filed out through the door sobbing loudly. The room was now left to the men, who had been praying elsewhere. They went to pay their last respects in a silent but similar way, after which the three elderly ladies returned and wrapped Hadduma's body in the family shroud. The shroud is taken off the body at the moment of burial.

As her kinsmen carried her through the door, the same one through which she had been carried as a bride only fifteen years previously (before going to live with Muhand at r-'Attaf), the women's sobs turned to a piercing wail which rose in a crescendo until, slowly and solemnly, the bier with its retinue of male mourners disappeared from sight down the slope of the path. The cemetery lay halfway between r-'Attaf and l-'Ass and was a spread of rough land with bushes and trees growing on it and vaguely demarcated by stones placed here and there. A nice place to rest, I thought.

With the departure of the corpse the keening, hair-tearing and shrieking stopped, though the rest of the day was spent with more restrained tears—at least well simulated if not genuine—and mourning. The mourning observance lasts three days and women from households not closely connected with the bereaved family take over the essential chores of the house and do the cooking. All that day women formed groups and discussed Hadduma's virtues, interspersed with moans of "aiee, aiee, aiee" and heavy sighs. Once again I became the outsider and was glad to slip away unobtrusively to the quietness of our room, where I found Dave. He too had felt himself *de trop* among the men. The harrowing ritual of preparing the body, washing it and scenting it that I had witnessed stayed in my thoughts for days.

Hadduma's demise served to speed our departure and we left l-'Ass the following day. To lighten the mood, for we all felt sad, I promised I would be back, perhaps in a month or so. We all pretended to believe it—for who can predict the Will of God?

The ladies thronged around the door and 'Aisha balanced me as I scrambled from the bank onto the slippery mule paniers. Dave and Muhand were waiting for me and in single file we rode forlornly down the trail. I glanced back at that friendly old house and at its inmates who had been so kind to me and gave them a final wave, and then we were out of sight.

Back in Muhand's house, removed from the tragedy, poor Hadduma's death receded into the background and life was resumed as normal. There was no sign of Hmid and no great concern was shown; obviously he could look after himself. Then, a few days later, he appeared from nowhere looking thinner than ever, tired and silent. There was an altercation between Muhand and his mother, but she had her way and two of the daughters were designated to tend the goats for a while so that Hmid would not be on his own to brood. Arhimu gave him hard jobs to do nearer home and kept him running errands till he began to pick up again.

But our days of fieldwork, too, had come to an end—as much as fieldwork can ever come to an end—and it was time to return to the hustle of our society, and that saddened me. The morning finally arrived when the family and friends helped us to pack the Land Rover while Muhand's mother hovered around with her grey, wispy hair sticking out from under her turban and tried to keep the smaller children from getting underfoot. I sipped a final glass of tea with Khadduj, Rwazna and Yamna. We were determined to be gay, but our forced jokes and smiles fell flat and it was with a sense of relief that Muhand's imperious honking on the horn brought us to our feet.

Arhimu ran in: "Munat! the men are waiting; it is time to go." The moment of departure had arrived. The ladies accompanied me to the massive door. I said goodbye to Arhimu first; she kissed me and hugged me tightly, dabbing at her eyes. And as she pushed me from her she shoved into my hands an earthernware pot that I had admired long ago, in which she kept almonds. My determination to remain cheerful wavered; I turned to the three other young women but suddenly their faces crumpled and at the sight of their tears my own reserve vanished and we kissed each other goodbye with wet and tear-stained cheeks. Then I stumbled through the door and into the Land Rover. Muhand looked startled, then gunned the motor and Dave, without a word, handed me his handerchief. I blew my nose loud and long into the outsize hankie, while Dris screamed in fury at not being allowed to accompany us. From the river bed we looked up at Muhand's house, but all we could see was the solid, closed door to the courtyard hiding from view the women and the life that buzzed within its confines.

When we reached Suq al-Arba‘, Hmid was already waiting with the mule for his father to ride back. We did not prolong the agony of our farewells in the marketplace, which was once again as deserted as the first day I had arrived there.

Silently we drove along the narrow, twisty unpaved road. Dave stared straight ahead. What was there to say? We both felt the same and wondered when, if ever, we would go back to that particular corner of the Rif: a corner which had meant so much to us, not only in the obvious terms of anthropological fieldwork but, far more, in the deeper terms of initially reserved but soon genuinely friendly and warm human contacts, relationships and problems.

16

Epilogue

After our departure from the Rif at the end of Dave's fieldwork late in the summer of 1965, we did not revisit the region for nearly twenty-two years, until March of 1987. We were well aware that major changes were taking place in the interim, some of them already perceptibly underway even while we were in the field; but nothing prepared us for the almost traumatic degree of culture-shock we experienced when we actually returned to the area two decades later. It is worth leading up to this final visit by painting in with broad strokes some of what had happened in the interim.

Any anthropologist knows that the end of his/her fieldwork is near when he/she starts to get noticeably diminshing returns in his/her information from both interviews and observation—and Dave had put in four full years of field time in the Rif, two in his bachelor days and two afterward with me. This was almost four times as long as the stint of the usual anthropological fieldworker. But as early as 1964, Muhand had been telling him how anxious he was to join the "gravy train" of migrant Rifian labor in Western Europe, and he enlisted Dave's help in obtaining a Moroccan passport. This proved to be no easy task, as the Moroccan authorities at the time were very suspicious of their own people. The Rifians, as a group, headed the list of suspects, particularly after the Aith Waryaghar revolt of 1958-59.

Furthermore, Muhand's police dossier, from the mere fact of his having worked with Dave, was already full to bulging. But somehow, by the time Dave and I moved to Spain at the end of 1967, all the wheels were in motion and we met Muhand off the boat in Malaga on his first trip to Europe early in 1968. He was on his way north, first to France and then to Holland—in both of which he had kinsmen and friends—to look over the opportunities for migrant Moroccan labor.

Just as the Rifians had been the first Moroccan labor migrants to colonial Algeria, to work on the farms of French settler-colons in Oran and its hinterland in the mid-nineteenth century (a source of employment cut off completely by Algerian independence in 1962), so also were they the first to start exploring, as early as 1960, the new job opportunities in Western Europe. France, Belgium, Holland and West Germany all needed workers, and by 1970 the trickle of labor migrants had grown into a flood.

Between 1968-69 and 1985—when he retired after the death of his hundred-year-old mother—Muhand would appear on our doorstep in Spain, alone or with friends or relatives, on the average of about once a year. He would stay for a night or two, either on his way to the Rif on holiday or back up to his job in Holland. After an initial two months exploring and then rejecting France, he had found work in Gouda, first in a biscuit factory and then later as a foreman in a milk-bottling plant. He was evidently quite pleased and satisfied with his job, and had been enterprising enough to learn Dutch.

Every time Muhand passed through he gave us all the latest news from home. One of the persistent themes in this news was the gradual change in the rural Rifian landscape through ever-increasing urbanization. The market centers that we had known previously in the Aith Waryaghar territory were now well on their way to becoming towns.

Although a handful of Rifian workers in Europe have their wives and children with them on the job (where adequate housing is available), the great majority are led by the ingrained tradition of female seclusion to leave their wives at home. Muhand was one of the latter, but by the mid-1970s his third wife, Khadduj, had died, and his two eldest sons, Hmid and Dris, were married. Through kinsmen in France he secured a job for Dris in Toulouse, and he found work for Hmid in Gouda, where they shared an apartment. Muhand himself was not to remarry again for several years, and we shared his loneliness and bereavement over the loss of Khadduj. But by now he had thirteen or fourteen children, the older ones of whom could now help to care for him. And every time he passed through Spain—usually in a late-model Toyota or Opel—we learned that more of his children had been married off.

It was probably the death of his hundred-year-old mother in mid-1985 that prompted the retirement of Muhand that year. He telephoned us to say that he was now on his way back to the Rif for good, and that we were more than welcome to come and stay with him at any time. He promised that he would literally kill the fatted calf and put on a great show, just as in the old days. We took him at his word, and eventually prepared—with some misgivings—to return to the Rif for a brief stay in March of 1987.

Dave's main purpose in making the trip was to photocopy and translate a document in Arabic, a *shajara* or justificatory family tree establishing Muhand's tribal pedigree (as well as his matrilateral descent from the Prophet Muhammad), with which he had been presented by the Ministry of the Interior in Rabat in about 1981. Muhand had already given Dave considerable verbal information about this document, and Dave was keenly interested in photocopying, transcribing and translating it, to form part of a corpus with other, considerably earlier, Rifian documents (many of which Muhand had also previously loaned him) that he was putting together for publication. And Muhand had agreed enthusiastically.

After sending Muhand a telegram warning of our impending visit, we drove east from Tangier to El Hoceima in the course of our next Moroccan trip. At Ktama we ran into a thick fog—as well as numerous youths who wanted to sell us *kif,* or hashish, the major produce of the region, which is legal to grow but not to sell! We did not arrive in El Hoceima until dusk, three hours behind schedule; the modernization since our last visit had not reduced the number of potholes in the road.

But almost everywhere we noted changes which alarmed and saddened us. Houses in the region had never previously been higher than one or two stories, but now four- and even five-story apartment buildings seemed to exist in every market center. In most cases they looked unplanned, having been placed here, there and everywhere, although not along anything resembling an urban grid. The open refuse dumps were appalling. The inspiration for these family-size apartment buildings had obviously come back from Europe with migrant laborers, but necessary utilities such as water, plumbing and electricity were rudimentary.

We had specified in our telegram that we would meet Muhand in a particular café in El Hoceima, one we both knew well, the following day at noon. We waited there until three o'clock in the afternoon, but he never appeared. This was not necessarily cause for alarm, as Moroccans tend to be casual about both keeping appointments and answering their mail. There was of course no way to reach him on the telephone, so that same day we set out for Suq al-Arba' Tawrirt. Along the way, we were dismayed to see even more of the new-style high-rises in Imzuren (which had become virtually a cement jungle of them) and Bni Bu 'Ayyash. At our destination we found out at the local post office that the Nkur River was still in flood from torrential rainstorms so that we could not possibly drive up to r-'Attaf or l-'Ass to see my old friends. We also learned that Muhand, for the past six months or so, had been living with his youngest son downriver in Bni Bu 'Ayyash in one of the many new apartments there. And yes, he had received and signed for our telegram.

So we backtracked to Bni Bu 'Ayyash, and through some older men who remembered Dave from his initial fieldwork in the region we finally located both the apartment block and the son (who was yet still younger than any of those whom we remembered). The boy told us that his father had gone to Ajdir and El Hoceima for the day, but would probably be back within an hour or so. There was nothing to do but wait in a café and have tea, which we did for another two hours before Muhand at last roared up in a nearly new Mercedes. He greeted us jocularly and said he would run us back to El Hoceima, where he would meet us at noon the next day. He had received our telegram but he shrugged it off, and there was no invitation to come in for tea or a meal. This was an unheard-of lack of hospitality on the part of a Moroccan; normally, even if it is three o'clock in the morning, the women are roused to get up, and the production of food of some sort and mint tea is *de rigueur.*

Muhand's whole manner was very offhand, while Dave and I did our best to make it clear that we were far more interested in seeing our old friends—and Muhand's kinsmen—upriver than in meeting the new Moroccan officialdom in Ajdir and El Hoceima. Muhand responded that at the moment any trip upriver was manifestly impossible. But the way he brushed aside the suggestion made us begin to wonder; and during the following week that we were to remain in El Hoceima we came to wonder even more.

However, Muhand did turn up at our hotel at the appointed time the next day, as promised, and took us to lunch. But he was a bundle of nervous tension, and did not eat a bite himself. He looked continuously at his watch, getting more anxious by the minute. Dave ignored his rudeness and explained that the main reason for our return was to get a copy of Muhand's *shajara* document for inclusion in the corpus of Rifian documents he was assembling for translation and publication. Muhand blithely agreed, but nothing came of it. He failed to bring the document to our meeting a day or so later, and when Dave asked about it again he said that he had left it in Rabat to be framed. All this time he was smoking furiously, tapping his fingers on the table, and jiggling his knee up and down. On the several further occasions we saw him during the week we were there, he would suddenly jump up and end the meeting by announcing that he had to rush off and see somebody. He was clearly giving us the brush-off.

On our last day in Bni Bu 'Ayyash, Muhand was waiting for us outside the café at the main road. He volunteered to go down to Rabat—where he said he had to go on business anyway—pick up the framed document, and then pass through Tangier three days later to give it to Dave at our hotel for photocopying. Of course, he never showed up at all. This was the end for us, particularly after our week of nearly total frustration in El Hoceima (although it had been good to see many old friends there).

It was only after our visit that we began to suspect what might well have been the reason for Muhand's exceptionally strange and erratic behavior toward us: that he was taking drugs. We reflected that his mannerisms had shown unmistakable drug symptoms, especially his extreme nervousness and consciousness of time. He may well have been heavily involved in overseeing the transport of "hash," of which Morocco has become a major world center. His friends were reticent in their comments, saying merely that Holland had changed him a great deal, and it was obvious that most of them avoided him when he was in town in El Hoceima. Dave later sent him one or two letters, but he never replied. And so, with great sadness on our part at least, an old friendship has come to an end.

I was, of course, not taken to see any of the women in his family, even those of my own present age, or to note possible changes in attitudes among them. (The old *aya-ralla-buya* music and dances, for example, have been modernized with electronic guitars.) Instead, I was taken and dropped near the lowland women's market, where—except for one old lady who recognized me and jumped up to give me a welcoming hug, scattering the goods placed on boards all around her—the girls were giggly or insolent, and scornful of my much-forgotten Rifian. So after a few minutes I left, feeling self-conscious and embarrassed.

Widespread labor migration has produced the temporary, or occasionally even permanent, breakup of nuclear families. Deserted wives sometimes see their friends accompanying their husbands to the bright lights of Europe. Those young women come back emancipated, and no doubt they gossip spitefully about the goings-on of the absent husbands, some of whom they report as having married foreign women who are unaware of another wife (or wives) or children in Morocco. This leads to jealousy and discontent among the wives left at home.

We saw many of the young men without employment—or even the desire to find it—lolling around in cafés, waiting for their fathers' money orders to arrive. Those who did not look too ragged occasionally had the luck to pick up female tourists looking for fun and willing to spend money.

It is also quite possible that some of the undeniable power that women wield behind the scenes in the Rif, especially as they get older and more established as mistresses of households and then as mothers-in-law, may be coming further front and center. Women have technically had the right to vote ever since the first major parliamentary elections in the post-independence period in 1960, but until very recently they have been blocked from doing so by their menfolk, who regard political participation as purely a male prerogative (even though they themselves have often been indifferent about exercising it in the post-colonial period).

In spite of the money invested in the region from the savings of returnee labor migrants, unemployment is still high, as is overpopulation. With the exodus of men to work in Europe, traditional agriculture has almost completely died on the vine. (This might have happened in any case through extended overuse of an infertile soil.) Finally, the reportedly high usage of drugs in the region does not help matters.

Here and there, though, one can spot signs of at least a certain external prosperity (Muhand's Mercedes, for instance, or the recent emphasis on gold jewelry as a form of security in the El Hoceima shops). But the traditional debt structure survives.

So despite the revenues returning from labor migration, intractable problems bedevil the Rif: poverty, overpopulation, declining agricultural productivity, weakened family cohesion and drug use. Such elements in combination make for a potentially explosive sociopolitical situation.

Meanwhile, Dave and I are doing our best to blot out the memory of that disagreeable final week. In our older years, we prefer to remember "our Rif" as it was during the wonderful days of fieldwork.

About the author . . .

URSULA KINGSMILL HART was born in 1920 of British parents in south-central India. She was educated in France in the French lycée system and grew up in Morocco, the country that she has always considered her home. She joined the British Services and spent the Second World War years in England, returning to Morocco in 1958. There she met her American anthropologist husband, David Montgomery Hart, and accompanied him on most of his extensive and intensive field trips throughout that country. She has three children from a previous marriage living in various parts of the world, while she and her husband currently live in the Almería province of southeastern Spain. She has previously published *Two Ladies of Colonial Algeria: The Lives and Times of Aurélie Picard and Isabelle Eberhardt,* Ohio University Monographs in International Studies, Africa Series, No. 49 (Athens: University of Ohio Press, 1987).

Suggestions for Further Reading

Ahmed, Akbar S., and David Montgomery Hart, eds. *Islam in Tribal Societies: From the Atlas to the Indus*. London: Routledge and Kegan Paul, Ltd., 1984.

——. *Muslim Tribal Societies in Colonial Ethnography: Readings from Morocco and Pakistan*. London: Routledge, forthcoming.

Coon, Carleton S. *Tribes of the Rif,* Harvard African Studies, IX. Cambridge, MA: Peabody Museum, 1931.

Hart, David Montgomery. *Emilio Blanco Izaga: Colonel in the Rif,* Ethnography Series, HRAFlex Books MX3-001, 2 vols. New Haven: Human Relations Area Files, Inc., 1975.

——. *The Aith Waryaghar of the Moroccan Rif: An Ethnography and History,* Viking Fund Publications in Anthropology No. 55. Tucson: University of Arizona Press, 1976.

——. *Documents from the Moroccan Rif.* Wisbech (Cambridgeshire): MENAS Press, and Tetouan: Université de Tetouan, 1994, in press.

——. *Traditional Society and the Feud in the Moroccan Rif.* Wisbech (Cambridgeshire): MENAS Press, and Rabat: Faculté des Lettres et des Sciences Humaines, Université Mohammed V, 1994, in press.

——. *Qabila: Tribal Profiles and Tribe-State Relations in Morocco and the Afghanistan-Pakistan Frontier.* Wisbech (Cambridgeshire): MENAS Press, and Rabat: ISESCO, forthcoming.

Pennell, C. R. *A Country with a Government and a Flag: The Rif War in Morocco, 1921-1926.* Wisbech (Cambridgeshire): MENAS Press, 1986.